In all of my forty-two years of ministry I've not seen anyone with a more vibrant faith and fury. Cora has such conviction and a relentless, bulldog faith that it seems to combust into an explosion of dogged tenacity when she is under attack. Her church, her family, and the enemy have come to respect her ability to go to war for the promises of God! Reading her book will transform the timid and invigorate the tenacious to become ferocious warriors with every turn of a page! My daughter has totally redefined what it means to fight like a girl!

—T. D. JAKES SR.
SENIOR PASTOR, THE POTTER'S HOUSE OF DALLAS

Cora Jakes Coleman takes readers on a transparent and bold journey. *Ferocious Warrior* compels the reader to go beneath the surface of prayer, discernment, and warfare. The fire of God resides in this book! Your life will never be the same.

—MARANDA CURTIS
GOSPEL SINGER

Cora has been with me through some of my scariest fights and has always fought ferociously with faith and prayer for me. I have no doubt that her book *Ferocious Warrior* will not only inspire you to rise, but it also will make you feel what I have felt having Cora in my life. Cora doesn't just throw you in the fight; she teaches you how to fight and she fights with you. I can honestly say I've never seen a more ferocious prayer warrior than my Coco Bean. Get ready for a great read.

—TAMAR BRAXTON
SINGER, SONGWRITER, TV PERSONALITY

Ferocious Warrior is uplifting and relatable. It is a must read and a blueprint for those looking for ways to strengthen their faith and prayer life. It is an experience.

Cora Jakes Coleman is a battle-ready, devil-stomping warrior ready to lead this generation with a ferocious word from God.

—LeToya Luckett-Walker
Grammy Award–Winning Singer

CORA JAKES COLEMAN

FEROCIOUS
Warrior

CHARISMA
HOUSE

Most CHARISMA HOUSE BOOK GROUP products are available at special quantity discounts for bulk purchase for sales promotions, premiums, fund-raising, and educational needs. For details, write Charisma House Book Group, 600 Rinehart Road, Lake Mary, Florida 32746, or telephone (407) 333-0600.

FEROCIOUS WARRIOR by Cora Jakes Coleman
Published by Charisma House
Charisma Media/Charisma House Book Group
600 Rinehart Road
Lake Mary, Florida 32746
www.charismahouse.com

Library of Congress Cataloging-in-Publication Data:
An application to register this book for cataloging has been submitted to the Library of Congress.
International Standard Book Number: 978-1-62999-659-2
E-book ISBN: 978-1-62999-660-8

19 20 21 22 23 — 987654321
Printed in the United States of America

I DEDICATE THIS BOOK TO YOU. Yes, you, the person reading this right now. I dedicate this book to everyone who picks this book up in hopes of becoming a ferocious warrior in prayer. I dedicate this book to you because if it weren't for your heart toward me and the many prayer requests I have received, I wouldn't have written this book at all. I am grateful for you. I pray this book trains you, teaches you more about yourself, and helps you know you are not alone. Life can be hard, and I pray you use this book as a tool to help you get through your ugly fights. Remember, I am fighting with you and all will be well. So here's to you becoming ferocious and dismantling your enemies.

I also dedicate this book to my family—my husband, father, mother, sisters, and brothers who never stifled my dreams or my prayers but have always supported me. Finally, I dedicate this book to Jason and Amauri, my "first babies." Mommy is so proud of who you are becoming and have become for the kingdom. I fought for both of you and would do it all over again. You are both going to be amazing.

Thank you for grabbing this book. I pray it blesses you.

Contents

Foreword

OVER THE YEARS there have been many words that have crossed my mind when attempting to define my sister, Cora Jakes Coleman. In my life her roles have fluctuated between best friend, beloved adversary, protagonist, partner in crime, tutor, babysitter, number one supporter—the list goes on and on. But as we have both emerged into the fullness of womanhood, there is one role she has consistently embraced with power and authority: prayer warrior.

When I was just a little girl whose timid prayers were laced with insecurity and doubt, my sister would pray with said power and authority until it forced my unvoiced skepticism into divine submission. I believe her commitment to prayer has been the hum that pulled our family through troubled waters.

Simply stated, Cora prays for heaven to touch earth. She could rightfully and decidedly choose to become the type of person people come to when they need someone to carry a prayer to God's ear, but she has chosen to expand heaven's ability to touch earth by depositing within each of us the knowledge and technique necessary for us all to war with prayer.

There will be moments in your life when it seems you have exhausted all possible resources. Those are the times when you must choose either to give in to the temptation to acquiesce to a life of despair and darkness or to fight until the flicker of hope in your soul becomes the light at the end of the tunnel.

In a world where stability is fleeting, it is imperative you discover and master the power that exists within your own mouth to declare anointed truths over your finances, relationships, health, spirituality, children, and wellness. The experiences of life are not meant to leave you stagnant but rather to create the necessary pressure required for you to emerge as a renewed and restored being.

This journey will challenge you to address your patterns, modify your vocabulary, and stretch your faith like never before. Cora will skillfully equip you with the tools necessary for you to engage in battle with everything that is waging war on who God has called you to be. No longer will you be on the sidelines watching, hoping someone will send out a prayer on your behalf, but you will engage actively with the miracle you need.

When you become the access point that allows heaven to touch earth in your world, you will witness glory like never before. Generational blessings and breakthrough are waiting to be released from the depths of your being, but heaven is looking for a specific sound. God needs vessels who are willing to walk away from what they think they know so they can see clearly what God is doing.

Prayer brings God's vision into focus and our frustrations to the surface. Prayer awakens our spirits when life has become difficult. Prayer is gasoline that sets our souls on fire. Prayer is the pavement on which we rest when God orders our steps. Believers who do not understand the power of prayer have not seen the fullness of their potential.

I am so glad you have decided not to live life blindly but with power, authority, and anointing. Your greatest weapon is not just in what you put in your mind but in how you release what you have learned into the atmosphere. The world will become better because of what you release as a result of reading this book.

—Sarah Jakes Roberts
Author, *Don't Settle for Safe* and *Lost and Found*
Co-pastor, The Potter's House at One LA
and The Potter's House of Denver

Introduction

"IS HE CASTING out a demon? That is absolutely amazing." Those were the thoughts that raced through my mind and leaped into my heart as I watched my father pray for someone who had suddenly started screaming and writhing uncontrollably. I was just a little girl, maybe six or seven years old, and it was the first time I remember ever seeing my dad pray like *that*. His voice boomed with an authority that demanded the demon get in alignment with the words he spoke. Yet I could sense so much love in his voice for the person seeking freedom. It was one of the most incredible moments I had ever witnessed—and not because the person made such a scene. It was because after my father prayed, the screaming and squirming ceased.

When I was growing up, my father, Bishop T. D. Jakes, reminded me of a big, ferocious bear. Week after week I saw my ferocious bear of a father fight hard, ugly battles so people could be set free from bondage and live in the fullness of God's purpose for them. Women were loosed, men were empowered, and youth were set on fire for Jesus because my father wasn't afraid to contend with the enemy.

I remember as a little girl seeing people roar and flex their bodies in ways that seemed humanly impossible as they cried out from the inside for a freedom only God could provide. Without hesitation my father would go running toward the person and begin to pray so he or she could experience deliverance. I watched both my father and mother use the power of prayer, faith, worship, fasting, sacrifice, and suffering to war not only for our family but also for the world.

During one service there was a woman in the sanctuary who was demon-possessed, and she seemed to be scaring everyone in the congregation, give or take a few. My father and mother stood there without even a hint of fear. My mother prayed as my father calmly spoke to the demon and told it to leave.

I was mesmerized by my parents' reaction to the woman. In that moment, I realized that if we have the power to believe Him, God can tear down any obstacle we face. When people say prayer is powerful, they aren't just repeating a cliché. God has given us keys to destroy the works of the enemy. We simply need to know how to use them.

That is why I have written this book. The enemy would like nothing more than for you to remain on the level you are, stuck in relationships that are not helping you grow, and doubting God's ability to move in your situation. The enemy would like nothing more than for you to believe the lies people have spoken over you and refuse to own the truth of who God says you are. But you have made the enemy mad because you picked up this book.

In these pages I have the privilege of sharing with you what I have learned about becoming a ferocious warrior. Ferocious warriors are ferocious in prayer, yes, but knowing how to pray is only part of being a ferocious warrior. Ferocious warriors know their purpose in God and are determined to pursue it. Ferocious warriors face their enemies without fear because they know that if God is for them, it doesn't matter who is against them.

Ferocious warriors find strength in surrendering to God and know that the biggest blessings often come after the greatest pain. They choose faith over fear and refuse to run from life's obstacles because they realize that pain and problems prepare us for our next level.

YOU ARE A THREAT TO THE ENEMY

I want to let you in on a little secret. The enemy is afraid of you. Now, he's not afraid of the person who lives under a cloud of doubt, fear, shame, bitterness, anger, and insecurity. He's afraid of the person you would become if you ever let those things go.

Fortunately I was never so naive as to think I wouldn't have any problems in life. Nothing—and I mean *nothing*—could be further from the truth. If you read my first book, *Faithing It*, you know I have struggled with infertility and have had to fight hard to become a mother. I have wrestled with depression and low self-esteem. I have had to overcome the pain of emotional, sexual, and physical abuse. I have experienced betrayal and heartbreaking loss. The battles I have fought have not been easy; in fact, some of them have been downright ugly.

My posture as a ferocious warrior did not come from places of luxury and happiness. Don't get me wrong; I was exposed to great blessings in life while growing up. But even my birth was a result of my parents' ferocious prayers. The enemy has tried many times to destroy me and my ability to be fruitful. From sickness and disease to depression, deception, and temptation, the enemy has tried countless times to kill me. And he has tried to get me to kill my hopes, my dreams, my aspirations, and even my expectations.

Maybe you can relate. If so, I have good news for you: the enemy never shakes your life up and fights you unless you are a threat to him.

I realized from a young age that if I did not learn how to defeat the enemy, he would take everything I held dear. So I learned how to fight, and when the fight got ugly, I got ferocious. When something is ferocious, it is extremely intense. The dictionary says *ferocious* means "exhibiting or given to extreme fierceness and unrestrained violence and brutality."[1] I am here to show you how you can become a ferocious force against the enemy and win even the ugly fights.

My first book, *Faithing It*, was about my journey to believe what God said despite the doctors' reports. *Ferocious Warrior* is about how I have fought for everything God wants to birth in me, physically and spiritually, and how you can do the same.

Your fight may not be like mine. I wanted to become ferocious after facing one ugly battle after another, from failed fertility treatments to adoption woes to staggering betrayals. Your fight may be a cancer diagnosis or a child who is acting crazy. It may be a marriage that is struggling or a faith that is faltering. Your fight may be in public, with even strangers making unwelcome comments on social media. Or you may be fighting quietly, shedding silent tears that no one ever sees. Whatever your fight looks like, you're not alone. I am fighting with you. I am here to share what I've learned and show you how to become a ferocious force against the destructive tactics of the enemy.

In these pages you will discover how to build ferocious faith and develop a consistent, disciplined walk with God. You will learn how to recognize the tactics of the enemy and dismantle doubt, fear, sorrow, low self-esteem, anger, bitterness, grief, and anything else he uses to keep you from becoming the best version of yourself—the person God created you to be. You will gain insights that encourage you to become passionate and persistent in prayer, as well as to get out of your own way so you can move to your next level in God.

But where would warriors be without their weapons? You have a myriad of weapons at your disposal, and I want to help you discover them. God's Word is a weapon, your faith is a weapon, and your worship is a weapon, and I want to help you learn to use each one more effectively. You may have been battling for years, but this time you don't have to go it alone. I am here to speak to your spirit about how you can grow as a force against the enemy, take your power back, and defeat what is trying to destroy you.

Yet more than anything, I want to help you deepen your relationship with the One who strengthens you in the fight and gives you the power to overcome even in the face of insurmountable odds. The God we serve is all-powerful.

At the end of each chapter there is a prayer modeled after the ones that helped me become a more ferocious warrior. Use those prayers to speak into your situation. You can even imagine me there praying with you, because I am praying for you.

I have also included affirmations and related scriptures at the end of each chapter for you to declare throughout your day. Years ago the Holy Spirit told me not to say anything I couldn't back with Scripture. So I've not only given you affirmations but also the scriptures that support them. Post those truths on your bathroom mirror, in your car, at your desk at work—wherever you will see them throughout the day. Keep declaring them until they go deep in your heart and mind and change what you believe about yourself. In appendix B you will find additional scriptures and declarations that can be used during times of prayer.

Now, I must warn you: this book is going to cause things in your life to shift. You are going to become better because you have chosen to tap into the power that will cause your life to change. You are designed to be fruitful, and the enemy wants nothing more than to destroy your ability to produce. He wants to keep you from discovering the strategies that will empower you to face your enemies without fear and destroy their hold over your life. But it's your time to buck against the enemy. This is your moment to finally become who you are called to be—a ferocious warrior. Are you ready?

CHAPTER 1

Ferocious Faith

MY NAME IS Cora Jakes, and when I grow up, I am going to be a preacher just like my daddy." Those were the words of a five-year-old girl. I didn't know then that I was planting seeds into my destiny, but I became a daughter of faith and declaration that day. Since then I have lived my life by faith, and I can tell you, it is no easy walk. But you cannot become a ferocious warrior without ferocious faith.

Ferocious faith believes God relentlessly and follows Him even into dangerous and uncomfortable places. It doesn't give in to fear and is the shield that protects the ferocious warrior. It is a bold, powerful faith that is not intimidated or overwhelmed by the enemy but instead makes him cower in fear.

When you have ferocious faith, you see victory instead of defeat. You have hope instead of shame. You believe what God says about you and not what others have said. When you have ferocious faith, you walk into uncharted territory and enter rooms you never thought you would access because God makes room for you. When you have ferocious faith, you make the enemy sorry he ever counted you out.

Ferocious faith is a fighting faith. I like to describe it as a "violent" belief in God. It is when your faith in God is so strong, so relentless, and so brave that it literally becomes a weapon to conquer the enemy. But this kind of faith doesn't just appear out of nowhere. To develop this kind of faith, you have to be willing to go through some hard times. In order to tap into ferocious faith, you have to consider it pure joy when you face fights that seem as if you are going to lose, because your strength is made perfect in the things that make you appear weak.

FACE YOUR FEARS

> God has not given us a spirit of fear, but of power and of love and of a sound mind.
> —2 TIMOTHY 1:7, NKJV

You cannot be ferocious if you are bound by fear. I sometimes think of ferocious faith as "first-responder faith," because it is the kind of faith that runs toward the obstacle instead of away from it. You will not become ferocious until fear becomes a stepping-stone and not a stumbling block.

Ferocious faith is built as you choose to stop living in the past, take hold of your vision, and refuse to let fear keep you from seeing your vision come to pass. I want you to become the best version of yourself, but you cannot do that if you constantly run from the fight. The things that scare you can either stop you or elevate you.

We all are trying in one way or another to move forward. We want to be in a different place from where we are right now. There is always something more to reach toward. How you respond to fear will determine whether you reach the place of victory. It is time to stop being afraid of the devil and start taking him down. You are too strong to be overwhelmed by a defeated foe. You are too strong to be a slave to fear. You are called to be ferocious.

Being ferocious means you have to stop being weak for the enemy. Yes, I said it! When you allow someone who is already defeated to take your power to overcome, you're being weak.

Don't let the enemy make you feel weak—start to bring weakness to the enemy.

Being ferocious may mean you have to release some things. When I decided to get ferocious, I had to let go of things that were hurting me and stop trying to be everyone's savior. I am a fixer, and at one time in my life I was always trying to make sure everyone's problems were solved and they were doing OK. But I did that at the expense of taking care of my own needs. I held on to relationships that were unhealthy and became the person others thought I should be instead of who I was called to be. I have learned you cannot let pleasing other people become more important than pleasing God. Ferocious warriors cannot worry about people's opinions. Your elevation to ferocious faith is going to come when you are ready to stop being broken by your fear and stand up to the inner enemy that says you aren't good enough.

You can be your own worst enemy. Being ferocious may mean resisting the voice that says you aren't going to make it, even if that voice is your own, and instead believing what God's Word says is true. "In all these things we are more than conquerors through him who loved us" (Rom. 8:37). Ferocious faith makes you resist social conventions and religious rules to reach for Jesus, just as the woman who had been subject to bleeding for twelve years did. According to the law of that time, she should not have been out in public, much less trying to touch the hem of Jesus' garment. But she believed Jesus could make her whole again, and the Bible says her faith made her well. (See Matthew 9:20–22; Mark 5:25–34; and Luke 8:43–48.)

Ferocious faith is so relentless, it makes you willing to stand in the lion's den, just as Daniel did, rather than compromise the truth. Ferocious faith is so confident in the faithfulness of God, it makes you willing to be thrown into a fire, just as Shadrach,

Meshach, and Abednego were, rather than bow to anyone or anything other than the one true God. Ferocious faith stands on the truth of God's Word: "Fear not, for I have redeemed you; I have called you by your name; you are Mine. When you pass through the waters, I will be with you; and through the rivers, they shall not overflow you. When you walk through the fire, you shall not be burned, nor shall the flame scorch you. For I am the LORD your God, the Holy One of Israel, your Savior" (Isa. 43:1–3, NKJV).

You were born to be ferocious because you were formed by a God who is ferocious. I challenge you to let the moments of fire, pressure, and pain grow your prayer life rather than paralyze you so you end up in sinking sand. The thing about faith is pressure helps build it. It cannot be built without pain and problems. You will experience many fights in life. No matter your gender, race, political views, or denomination, you will face obstacles. There is no way around that. What you can control is how you deal with the times in life that hurt you the most and what you choose to learn from them.

AVOID THE BLAME GAME

Being ferocious in your faith is about taking responsibility for where you are in life. If your vision has not become a reality, are you willing to make the choices necessary to change that? It would be easier to blame your mom, dad, cousin, auntie, neighbor, sister, brother, or even the bully from third grade for everything that has gone wrong in your life. But at the end of the day the only one who can truly keep you from moving toward what you desire in life is you.

You have to be willing to take responsibility for your life despite what you have been through. That is what it means to be ferocious. A large part of being ferocious is being able to admit you did something wrong and choose to make better decisions in the future. Most of your decisions do not directly affect anyone as much as they affect you. You may have been rejected, abandoned, neglected, overlooked, and ostracized by people, maybe even by family members, but that does not have to dictate how you view yourself right now. Whether you choose to love yourself is a decision *you* make; it is not a choice anyone makes for you.

You could spend your life saying the reason you are stuck or even broken is the person who hurt you or where you came from. But how does that account for who you are deciding to be today? When you consider your life, are you happy with who you are allowing yourself to be? Or have you let fear disable you?

Sometimes we make choices that keep us in painful situations. Having the humility and self-respect to accept our share of the responsibility for the pain we have experienced can be healing. I could have easily stayed depressed and broken for life, but staying broken and in pain would not have brought God glory, nor would it have helped me become the person I desire to be. Pain, crying, anger, losing things and people—believe it or not, they're all steps to success. I know this from experience. The life of faith can lead you into many different places, and I learned the most about faith when I was in the darkest place of my life.

FIGHT BACK

Choosing faith is hard, but for me it was easier than being beaten, blocked, and broken by fear. If you refuse to confront fear and you keep letting it dictate your actions, you will only get what fear can produce. Fear cannot produce effective faith; it can only dismantle it. Ferocious faith takes on fear, depression, anger, loneliness, marriage madness, motherhood woes, etc. like a champion boxer defending his title in front of thousands of people. Every fight you choose to face can help you become better. But don't think you can get in the ring with your greatest enemy without the fight getting ugly.

This is not a drill. The enemy has been after your faith since you were a baby, and you have to take your authority back. You may be thinking that is easier said than done. Well, let me help you by sharing a little of my story. At around the age of twelve or thirteen, I went through depression. As a young, brown-skinned girl, I didn't feel like I was pretty or even valuable. It wasn't that I didn't feel loved. My family and friends made me feel extremely loved. I just didn't love myself. I would look in the mirror and hate what I saw. I wanted to be lighter-skinned, taller, and more developed. Every day, my meeting with the mirror became more daunting, as I would find ways to hate myself more than the day before. It depressed me so much that I became comfortable in depression, so I began to find other ways to hate myself so I could continue in the depression and false sense of comfort.

I believe I attempted suicide at least three times during that season in my life. I was going to church, but I wasn't praying, reading my Bible, or truly being faithful to God's Word. I wasn't open to believing anything good someone said about me because I did not see the good in myself. I let insecurity become my security blanket. I know that doesn't make sense, but I became comfortable in my depressed, insecure state. Then I looked in the mirror one day and realized I had to make a different decision. I had to stop meeting up with depression like it was date night. I had to fight for my joy, my love, my peace, my healing, my hope, my endurance, and ultimately my power.

I let fear take what God had given me when He formed me in my mother's womb, and I had to fight to get my stuff back. No, depression didn't just pack up and leave overnight. It left when I started telling myself a different story—the story of what God said about me—and kept repeating it until I finally believed it. That is ferocious faith.

Ferocious faith causes you to challenge yourself to be a better person every day. You cannot get to your destiny without discipline. We often become the abuser in our own story because instead of loving ourselves, we find a way to hate ourselves. The prisons of fear and insecurity we find ourselves in are often built with the things we tell ourselves.

Romans 10:17 says that "faith comes by hearing, and hearing by the word of God" (NKJV). We develop ferocious faith by hearing the Word of God *and believing what it says*. What God's Word says may be vastly different from what we constantly tell ourselves. Too often we become our own worst enemy by refusing to let positive affirmations or encouraging words penetrate our hearts and minds so we can be transformed. Rather, we hold on to our victim status and then get mad when we don't get the victory.

You cannot believe in God and not believe what His Word says. Many people claim to believe in themselves, but they won't examine themselves and make the necessary changes to align their beliefs about themselves with what God's Word says. To be a ferocious warrior, you must be willing to make conscious decisions to become the best version of yourself. No matter where you are in your journey of faith, you should have at least a small desire on the inside to become the best version of yourself. There is absolutely no reason you shouldn't work to be the best you that you can be.

NO, IT'S *NOT* EASY!

Not once have I said the journey to becoming a ferocious warrior is easy, because it is not. It is hard to look at yourself and say, "No, I am the problem. I chose to hate myself, and if I can choose to hate myself, then I can choose to love myself." I couldn't blame anyone but myself for hating on me, and I couldn't blame anyone else for my insecurity. The blame belonged to me.

When I finally realized that, I got angry with myself. But I was so afraid of that emotion that I would bottle the anger inside and smile as if everything was OK, even though I wanted to scream at the top of my lungs. I went on like that for years, suppressing my anger and screaming on the inside. Then one day I realized I was pushing people completely out of my life. That is what can happen with any negative emotion we don't allow ourselves to process. It can become a wall that keeps everyone else out and traps us inside.

Ferocious faith was birthed when I was able to feel my anger, depression, pain, sorrow, and regret without falling into sin. The Bible tells us to be angry and sin not (Eph. 4:26). Man, that was hard, but I couldn't become ferocious against the enemy until I was able to become ferocious against the things making me reject myself. I battled infertility physically, but I mishandled the pain, and it eventually consumed me until I was nothing but a shell. Yet in that place of emptiness I learned that God is everything. And I learned the strategy of my enemy.

Depression, fear, anger, doubt, worry, loneliness—those are the enemy's favorite pieces to play. His strategy is to bring depression or some other negative emotion so you will get distracted and not activate your power in God. The enemy wants you to be consumed by confusion. He wants you to get comfortable in that dark place so you don't attempt to break out. Ultimately he wants you to forget about your light. But letting fear keep you from being ferocious toward the enemy ends today.

Today you will make a decision to stop looking in the mirror and hating who you are. Instead you will remember that you are "fearfully and wonderfully made" (Ps. 139:14) and take responsibility for where you are and make decisions that ultimately bring healing. This may require hard work on your part, and it may even bring some pain, but it will be worth it.

THE DOS AND DON'TS OF FAITH

The enemy uses the same strategy over and over: he tries to intimidate you. But when you have ferocious faith, you will intimidate him with your power. There is power in your ability simply to believe that what you desire to do in life is possible. You have a power in your faith that makes you ferocious to the enemy.

When your faith is ferocious, you can destroy the enemy's grip on you. You may lose some friends. You may lose some people you thought loved you. But it is all part of you gaining the intel for your fight. I am not here to make you comfortable—I am here to get you ready to fight back.

Sometimes when we feel as if we have been fighting, the reality is that we have not been fighting the right way. It is time for you to come out of your dead place and begin to have life and life more abundantly.

There is a type of faith that makes the enemy afraid of *you*. But before you can truly tap into that kind of faith, you must recognize what can cause your faith to falter. I call them the dos and don'ts of faith.

Don't doubt.

To doubt is "to call into question the truth of; to be uncertain or in doubt about" or "to lack confidence in."[1] Doubt is a lack of faith. When you are unstable in your convictions, your lack of confidence will show. A large part of walking by faith is walking in certainty. When you are uncertain, you open yourself up to being attacked by the enemy instead of using your faith to dismantle the enemy. You cannot use a weapon—or much less be a weapon—if you doubt your ability to do what seems impossible.

Let me tell you a story from Matthew 14 about how faith empowered a man to do the impossible.

You may remember the account of Jesus feeding the five thousand with just two fish and five loaves of bread. Bear in mind that the five thousand only accounted for the men; there were thousands more women and children. After miraculously multiplying a young boy's lunch, Jesus continued to minister to the people. Later He sent the disciples ahead of Him by boat to the other side of the Sea of Galilee while He dismissed the crowd and spent some time in prayer.

Shortly before dawn Jesus decided to meet up with the disciples, who were by that time a considerable distance from land. But this is Jesus we're talking about—the One who turned water into wine and just fed five thousand people with two fish and five loaves of bread. What's a little water to the Son of God?

I love the way the Bible puts what happened next: "Jesus went out to them, walking on the lake" (Matt. 14:25). It is written as if that kind of thing happens every day. But it's clear from the disciples' reaction that people didn't normally get across the Sea of Galilee on foot.

When the disciples saw Jesus coming toward them, they thought He was a ghost. Jesus told them not to be afraid, but that didn't calm them down. So Peter called out, "Lord, if it's you…tell me to come to you on the water" (Matt. 14:28). Jesus told him to come, and the Bible tells us Peter got out of the boat and began to walk on water.

One step at a time Peter moved closer to God. Then he began to doubt, and within seconds he began to sink. When Peter was no longer certain Jesus would keep him above water, he was no longer able to do the impossible. Fortunately Jesus was there for him and pulled him out of the water. Even when you doubt, God is with you. You have the power to believe God and not doubt, but even when doubt comes, you can pray and ask Jesus to help your unbelief. Jesus will walk with you on the water, and He will pull you up when you begin to sink.

The Book of James says, "The one who doubts is like a wave of the sea, blown and tossed by the wind" (1:6). The enemy wants to scare you out of trusting God because if he can keep you from believing who God is, he can cause you to lose your footing. I declare that every bit of doubt that tries to plague you as you are becoming ferocious will be demolished, never to return. I plead the blood of Jesus over your mind—that your mind would be anchored in the things that make faith easy. When you truly begin to dedicate yourself to prayer, worship, praise, and reading the Word, you will find that believing God becomes easy. And when you truly trust and believe God will never leave you to fail, faith becomes easy.

Don't be deceived.

James 1:16–18 reveals another don't when it comes to having ferocious faith. The passage tells us:

> Don't be deceived, my dear brothers and sisters. Every good and perfect gift is from above, coming down from the Father of the heavenly lights, who does not change like shifting shadows. He chose to give us birth through the word of truth, that we might be a kind of firstfruits of all He created.

It is easy to be deceived if you are not grateful for what God has already given. When you don't care for what you have, the enemy can deceive you into wanting more or dishonoring what you have been given. One of the first tests of faith is whether you can be faithful over what God has already given you.

You may be praying for a house, but can you praise God in your studio apartment? You may be praying for a nice car, but can you praise Him in your hooptie? We often pray for a companion but cannot be happy in the relationship when things aren't going the way we expect them to go. The Book of James reminds us to consider how we have postured our faith when it comes to being grateful.

Deception is beautiful and alluring, and if you aren't careful, it will take everything it can from you. Deception attracts your attention. It is incredibly dangerous because if you allow it to enter, it will cause you to detach from what sustains you. You cannot get in a habit of losing who you are because you've been deceived into thinking others know who you should be or what you should want. Deception isn't easily discerned by a heart that is broken and desiring love.

Sometimes we are easily deceived because we don't want to believe what we see and feel. Discerning deception is not an easy task. If it were, your fight wouldn't be as hard. Deception is a beautiful distraction that feeds your doubts. That's what happened to Adam and Eve. In the Garden of Eden, Eve had everything she could ever want or need, yet the serpent distracted her with his false claims. He made her think she didn't have everything she needed, and suddenly she began to doubt what she knew to be true. She began to think God was holding out on her and Adam, and what she had no longer seemed like enough. She lost her gratitude for what God had given her and bit into what the serpent fed her, and in doing so, she drew Adam into her deception. In Adam's love and, I believe, commitment to her, he received what she gave him, even though her decision would cause them to be sent out of paradise. Deception can push you out of your promised land, and it can cause you to miss out on what is good for you. Eve let a serpent deceive her and lost the wonderful gift God had given her. Instead of pleasure, she and Adam would become well acquainted with pain.

Don't just listen to the Word—do it.

James 1:22–25 tells us:

> Do not merely listen to the word, and so deceive your-
> selves. Do what it says. Anyone who listens to the word
> but does not do what it says is like someone who looks
> at his face in a mirror and, after looking at himself, goes
> away and immediately forgets what he looks like. But
> whoever looks intently into the perfect law that gives
> freedom, and continues in it—not forgetting what they
> have heard, but doing it—they will be blessed in what
> they do.

One of the hardest parts of being a ferocious warrior is following the Word of God and not allowing it to just be something you know but don't obey. How much sense would it make
to try to pass a college course without ever opening the textbook?
Yet that is how many people treat God's Word. They try to move
through life without knowing what God says about the situations
they face. You need to be able to study the Word and apply it so
your spirit can truly grow. Doing the Word is what causes you to
grow beyond your normal capacity. Again, it's not enough to read
the Word; it's important that you put into action what it says.

Don't give up.

Of all the don'ts we've discussed, the one I really want you to
consider is this: don't give up. Sometimes when you find yourself in an ugly fight, doubt will overcome you and suppress your
power, and in the process you lose yourself. Don't give up. Don't
lay down and die. There is strength in you. There is purpose in
you. The Word is in you. So don't give up. Take responsibility
for the times you stopped believing in God and what He can do
through you, and take your power back. Begin to affirm yourself

so you can step into new possibilities, "for at the proper time we will reap a harvest if we do not give up" (Gal. 6:9).

Do be quick to listen and slow to speak.

We have looked at several don'ts from the passage in James, but the dos are just as important. James 1:19–21 says: "My dear brothers and sisters, take note of this: Everyone should be quick to listen, slow to speak and slow to become angry, because human anger does not produce the righteousness that God desires. Therefore, get rid of all moral filth and the evil that is so prevalent and humbly accept the word planted in you, which can save you."

This passage tells us to be quick to listen and slow to speak. Sometimes you will learn the strategy of the enemy just by being quiet enough to hear the better way God is trying to reveal to you. Warriors who cannot listen before they speak are warriors who will never claim true victory. Consider what you speak. Anyone can talk, but not many people can say something that impacts others for the better.

You can change your situation just by thinking about what you say. Proverbs 18:21 says, "The tongue has the power of life and death." Your words can produce life or bring forth death in your relationships, your vision, and your future. When you aren't mindful of the things you say and do, you not only destroy yourself but also where you hope to go. Whatever course you choose, your mouth can affect where you go and how you get there.

Don't be religious.

Last but not least, don't be religious. Religion is not easy, but relationship with God is. Your religion is worthless if it is focused more on how things look than about who God is. A lot of people claim to be religious but carry judgmental attitudes and tear down people who don't fit the rules of their religion. Jesus did not come to proclaim the rules of religion; Jesus came because He loved us and wanted to have a relationship with us.

I learned how to fall more in love with Jesus when I laid aside religion and began to pursue a real relationship with God. I began to reach for Him, and I chose not to lose myself in anything but Him. It is one thing to know who you are. It is a completely different thing to know who is in you. Maybe you don't know if Jesus is in you. Let me tell you that you can be hurt, broken, and angry, but if you have accepted Christ as your Savior, God's power is in you. It's time to start unlocking that power.

A STRATEGY THAT FRIGHTENS THE ENEMY

To overcome depression, anger, shame, and embarrassment, I had to discipline myself in more than just prayer. I began to read the Bible and learn from the strategies the men and women in Scripture used to remain strong in faith as they endured the worst circumstances of their lives. Then I would pray for faith like that of Daniel, David, Deborah, or Naomi, and that faith began to frighten the enemy.

Walking in faith is easy when everything looks beautiful. But when pain strikes, it's hard to still say, "I have faith." When you are dealing with the symptoms of a condition you cannot change and the doctors don't know what to do, it's hard to have faith. When your friends betray you, it's hard to have faith. Developing ferocious faith takes vulnerability and discipline.

You are not alone in the journey to become the best version of yourself. I too am trying to become the best version of me. And I am still trusting God to send the children He showed me I would give birth to despite my struggles with infertility. This book is for my children who are yet to be born and for every person who has decided to stop living in fear, to walk ferociously toward the enemy, and to tear his territory down.

Faith is something that is developed; it is not something you just have. So strategize carefully. You cannot get to a place of success in life until you learn your strategy and your enemies. You cannot beat your opponent in a fight you don't have a strategy for. Some of the best fighters will tell you they didn't win the match because they could hit harder or move more quickly. They won because they had someone help them develop a strategy. So when you consider your life, have you considered your strategy? Keep in mind that ferocious faith doesn't come just from having a strategy; it comes when you discover God's strategy, found in His Word.

What you are going through right now—be it good or bad—is going to help develop a strength in you that frightens the devil. Whether your life has been filled with sorrow or joy, every experience helps develop your character. *Your pain is intel for your fight.* Your hurt is helping you figure out how the enemy hits you and how you can hit him back even harder. So "be on your guard; stand firm in the faith; be courageous; be strong" (1 Cor. 16:13).

You are a step closer to becoming ferocious, and I am so glad I get to help you prepare for your fight, develop a strategy against the enemy, and experience ferocious victory. As we close this chapter, I want you to take time to examine yourself. Reflect on who you are (see appendix A) and who you desire to be. Reflect on your life and the direction you desire to go. Think about what is pushing you to become ferocious.

A lot of what makes us ferocious is in our ability to pray no matter what the circumstances are. So I want to end this and every chapter with a prayer patterned after the ones I used during my journey to become a ferocious warrior. Pray it over yourself and add to it if you like, and expect God to endue you with ferocious faith.

You are not alone. I am fighting with you and for you. I am your faith coach, and we are going to win!

PRAYER FOR FEROCIOUS FAITH

Father God, I love You and I appreciate Your heart for me. I know it is going to take ferocious faith for me to become a ferocious warrior. I desire to dismantle the enemy and become the person You have called me to be. I am tired of losing things in life because I am too afraid to believe in You and have true faith. I appreciate Your hand over my life. I appreciate Your good thoughts toward me. But I confess, God, that I have had doubt and unbelief in my heart. I confess that at times I haven't felt like Your masterpiece. I confess that sometimes I have blamed You for things You didn't have anything to do with. I confess that I have seen myself as a victim and not victorious. I confess that I have been comfortable in sin when I should have been thirsting for You.

God, I thank You for all You have done in my life. I thank You for putting breath in my body and for making Your presence known to me. I thank You for tearing down strongholds in my life. I thank You for destroying the hand of the enemy over my life. I thank You for giving me wisdom that surpasses my understanding. I thank You for unmerited favor. I thank You for lifting up a standard on my behalf. I thank You for loving me enough to correct me when I am wrong. I thank You for being patient with me while I meet the expectations that You have for me and that I have for myself.

I pray, O God, that You would help me to consider what I say to others and what I allow others to say to me. I ask You to keep Your voice clear in my head and to keep me focused on the things making me fruitful and not filthy. God, I ask that You keep me from distractions.

I ask that You destroy generational curses of doubt and unbelief in my bloodline. I ask that You destroy every condemning strategy pointed in my direction. God, I ask that You increase and elevate my prayer life that I may walk boldly in who You have called me to be. I ask that You help me to see myself through Your eyes and to want You as much as You want me.

God, I ask that You teach me Your ways and let me not depart from them. Anchor me in the things that will bring forth the warrior in me. Awaken me in this season. Lord, I pray that You would help me not to doubt. Help me to discern what is trying to deceive me. Lord, help me to walk in the things that give me life more abundantly, and help me not to fall into the traps of the enemy.

I will not lose because I know You are with me. Train and guide me, God, to be and do what You have called me to be and do. Strip me of all unrighteous motives and lead me where Your grace is for my life.

I decree and declare that You died on the cross that I may be made new in You. I decree and declare that You are my Savior. I decree and declare that You have unhindered access to my heart, mind, and spirit from this day forth. I decree and declare that I am delivered from all dead things in my life and future. I speak fruitfulness over my life and over my family. In the mighty name of Jesus, it is so by faith, and by faith so it is. Amen.

Speak Life

So do not fear, for I am with you; do not be dismayed, for I am your God. I will strengthen you and help you; I will uphold you with my righteous right hand.

—ISAIAH 41:10

I don't have to fear as long as I have ferocious faith. I declare, according to Isaiah 41:10, that I will not fear because You are with me. I will not be dismayed because You are my God. You will strengthen and help me; You will uphold me with Your righteous right hand.

CHAPTER 2

The Gift From Betrayal

IF YOU ARE looking to be ferocious, the truth is you may have a different reason for wanting to become ferocious than I did. It may be a cancer diagnosis or a financial crisis. It may be a child who is addicted to drugs or a marriage that is in trouble. Ugly fights come in all shapes and sizes, and the fight—or should I say series of fights—that made me want to become ferocious came in the form of betrayal.

I have spent much of my life loving people and guiding them into purpose. I am very big on making sure people become the best possible version of themselves. I want those around me, especially close friends and loved ones, to become who God created them to be and see every dream He has placed in their hearts come to pass. But after thirty years I have learned that not everyone can receive what you have to give.

I am a nurturer by nature, so even at a young age I was always bringing people to my parents' house who did not have a healthy home life. If I had something, I wanted the ones I loved to have it too. I used to think that if I loved someone, that person was obligated to love me in return. Boy, was I wrong. I learned through a myriad of ugly fights that one of the strategies of the enemy is to set people in your life who will sit quietly, take from your table, smile in your face, and in the end betray you.

Now, it would be easy to call myself a victim, but I would be lying. I had family members and close friends who warned me several times about certain friendships. I hate to admit it, but almost every person my sister or best friend was uneasy about has hurt me in some way.

I may have been young, but I had spiritual children whom I poured my whole heart into. There was absolutely nothing I wouldn't give them if they needed it. I prayed for them, gave them money, and showed up anytime they needed something. But as soon as I started giving attention to someone else, it was as if everything I ever did for them became worthless, and they would suddenly end the friendship. I felt as if I were being punished for loving people by the very ones I poured most of my love into.

I'm sorry to say that for many people, dealing with betrayal will be part of the process of becoming a ferocious warrior. Often it starts after you pray for God to reveal who is for you and who is not. Have you ever prayed for God to expose something to you and then you start seeing changes in the people around you? This is God revealing to you who is for you and who is not.

I used to be devastated when people betrayed me, but I learned how to start thanking God for showing me who people truly were before I invested too much of myself into the relationship. Sometimes my prayer came too late and I experienced a lot of damage to my heart because I believed the best of people who never showed me they could be any better.

I expected people I had seen hurt others not to hurt me. Sometimes God gives you a seat in the front row of someone's life so you can see who the person truly is. If that person will lie, hurt, mistreat, and manipulate someone else, he or she will do it to you also. I am not saying you should trust no one. I am saying you should not let people take advantage of your kindness. Do not let people who are not trustworthy with others make you think you can trust them. Stop letting inconsistent people into your life and then getting upset when they don't meet your standards.

SOME RELATIONSHIPS WILL NEVER BEAR FRUIT

I have battled infertility openly. If you have read my book *Faithing It*, you know a car accident revealed large cysts on my ovaries and led to me having one ovary removed and being diagnosed with polycystic ovary syndrome (PCOS). I vividly remember the day the doctors told me it would be difficult for me to get pregnant. I can still feel the dampness from the tears that flowed down my face. I had never felt pain like that before in my life. I had wanted to be a mother since I was a little girl, so learning I would struggle to have children was devastating.

Since then I have gone through two rounds of in vitro fertilization (IVF), which led to a series of disappointments. Whenever my period was late, I thought I was going to receive the news I had been longing to hear only to find out I wasn't pregnant. I have fought and am still fighting hard against infertility, but I have learned that infertility goes beyond the physical. Some relationships are not productive, and they never will be. I have always wanted to be productive in every area of my life—in my friendships, in my marriage, in ministry...the list goes on. But I have come to realize that letting the wrong people get close to you can hinder your ability to produce.

How many people do you know who desire to produce things in life but are not productive at all? A person can have a business idea but not a plan, and that will keep him from making the idea a reality. A person can have a vision or dream but let the fear of failure, or even the fear of success, keep her from accomplishing it.

Whether you are male or female, when you have a "God idea" that you never bring to pass for one reason or another, you are being infertile. At its most basic level, infertility is simply an inability to produce, and it affects relationships as well as individuals.

Eventually I realized that I had infertile, or unproductive, friendships because I allowed the wrong people around me. I chose friends who consistently took from me and in the end betrayed me. As I searched for love in the wrong places, I let people get close to me who only wanted to take what I could give. I let people plant unfruitful seeds in my life by telling me I wasn't good enough, that I wasn't pretty enough, and that no one would ever love me. I let people plant seeds of doubt in my mind, and I began to accept what I should never have believed. I had to learn that if I let people plant dead seeds in my life, I would produce dead things. Having relationships that never grow is tied to letting dead things into your life.

I had to understand that infertility was not just affecting my body; it was and had been affecting my life and relationships for years. It did not start with the doctor's diagnosis when I was in my early twenties. Nor did it start with the needles and the process of IVF. It started when I began finding ways to hate myself as a little girl. It started when I allowed myself to believe I wasn't good enough.

As a preacher's kid one of the hardest things to find is loyal friends who don't want anything from you and will let you be yourself. I have been backstabbed by people who just weeks before would have called me their sister. I have been at the center of rumors. As a result I could have chosen to get sad and feel sorry for myself, but I have learned that when I go through things, I need to ask myself how the experience can make me better and how it will help me become the person I desire to be.

TAKE INVENTORY

A large part of self-discovery comes from taking inventory of how you ended up where you are. So that is what I did. I examined myself to see why I was letting people into my life who would hurt or sabotage me, and I learned it was because I was expecting people to meet a need in me that in reality only God could satisfy.

Sometimes when we are hurting, we allow other hurting people into our lives. But people who are hurting cannot help someone else who is hurting until they at least start the process of dealing with their own pain. I have learned that sometimes the best way to love someone who is wounded is to take yourself out of the equation so the person will have to lean on God and pray through the pain rather than get in a dysfunctional cycle that drains everyone involved. There are also times when the Holy Spirit will lead you to encourage and pray for someone. There are times when people who are wounded need someone to speak the truth in love to them or raise a shield of faith over them until they are strong enough to raise their own shield again. But I have brought people closer than they should have been and kept them in my life longer than they needed to stay because of a void I was trying to fill.

I used to place myself in relationships that would drain me financially because, truth be told, I believed the only way people would love me was if I was giving them money. I felt betrayed when the relationships ultimately went sour, but God used those experiences to help me recognize relationships that were one-sided. Now instead of trying to rescue people, I challenge them to create a plan to move toward what they want in life and then execute that plan by setting goals. Learning to set boundaries has helped me become ferocious.

When we decide to let God fill the voids in our lives, we will stop depending on people to pour into us and be strong for us.

Only God can truly satisfy and cause us to reach our fullest potential. The Book of Isaiah reminds us, "The LORD will guide you always; he will satisfy your needs...and will strengthen your frame. You will be like a well-watered garden, like a spring whose waters never fail" (58:11).

I believe in this season God is calling you to take responsibility for your choices. If you have been involved in relationships that are toxic, meaning you are letting people drain your strength and use you as a punching bag for their dysfunctional emotions, get out of those situations. When you allow God to fill you up instead of losing yourself in an unhealthy relationship, you will find strength to move toward the greater plan God has for you.

BETRAYAL CAN LEAD YOU TO GREATER

Although betrayal hurts, God can use it to bring something great into your life. My body betrayed me, but God was still faithful to make me a mother. My daughter's biological mother loved Amauri, but she wasn't able to care for her. So God brought Amauri into our lives so we could love, teach, protect, and raise her up to be who God would have her to be. Sometimes God uses other people to bring forth your promise.

Amauri came into my life after my first failed IVF cycle. I remember the first time I saw her picture and was told she was available to adopt. I was apprehensive because my daughter is half-Hispanic and half-black, and I didn't want her to feel out of place in our African American family. Little did I know God had already set us up for success.

My husband, Brandon, saw her picture and immediately knew she was our daughter. We went to pick her up at the agency to start the process of adopting a child from the foster care system, and as we were walking into the building, I tried to coach my husband and let him know Amauri wouldn't be leaping for joy to see us but would probably be scared. Again, little did I know God had set us up for success.

We walked in the door, and immediately Amauri ran up to me, jumped into my arms, and turned to the agent and said goodbye. Within minutes she was calling me and Brandon Mommy and Daddy. She received my family as if God had been showing her all along who we were. Amauri's birth name meant a gift from God, and her forever name also means a gift from God.[1] She truly has been a gift from God.

I never thought my fertility betraying me meant I wasn't worthy of gifts from God. This is often a misconception. Just because there may be areas in your life where you do not feel as if you are blessed does not mean you should count yourself out. God has already set you up for success. He has already set you up to win. There was no reason for Amauri to run to me as if she had known me for years. But sometimes being betrayed, broken, belittled, and bothered allows you to unlock the true blessing God has for you. I felt betrayed by my body when I was told I would struggle with infertility, but that betrayal opened the door for me to find my beautiful gifts from God, Amauri and Jason.

YOUR BLESSING IS WAITING

No matter what you've been battling, God has a plan to bless you. Jeremiah 29:11 says, "'For I know the plans I have for you,' declares the LORD, 'plans to prosper you and not to harm you, plans to give you hope and a future.'" You may be in a place right now where you feel like giving up. You may be feeling as if God has forgotten about you, and you aren't sure if He is ever going to answer your prayers. I want you to know that there is blessing waiting behind the hurt and betrayal. Your blessing is waiting behind that friend who used your pain against you. Your blessing is waiting behind that person who only saw what you could do for her and not the genuine love you had in your heart. I don't care how many rounds of IVF I went through; I would never have known God the way I do now if I had not gone through things that should have broken me.

If you have experienced the sting of betrayal, I have good news: there is a blessing waiting on the other side. So instead of avoiding the pain, embrace it. That is how betrayal or any other painful circumstance can help you develop into a ferocious warrior. Begin to show people the unconditional love of God. When you love people based on whether they meet your conditions, you are showing them your love, not God's. God's love sees the person behind the actions. When you can respond to those who hurt you in a Christlike, productive manner and show genuine compassion to them, you are demonstrating God's love, not your own. Your heart can deceive, but God's heart doesn't deceive. When you are showing God's heart, people should be able to see His attributes and character in you.

You can't win the ugly fights if you don't learn how to bob and weave through hurt and pain. What is going to activate the ferocious mindset in you is facing the things you would rather avoid. Pain is part of the formula to your power.

PAIN CAN BRING REVELATION

Friends and fertility betrayed me, but God never counted me out. Don't let your pain keep you from believing God still has a plan for your life that outweighs the hurt you have to endure to get there. Consider the example of Jesus.

Judas, one of the twelve disciples, betrayed Jesus for thirty pieces of silver. But Judas' actions led to Jesus' death on the cross, which brought redemption for you and me. I want you to think for a minute about times when God turned a painful experience around to bless you in some way. I know from experience that betrayal hurts in the beginning, but it brings revelation in the end. I learned to speak violent, devil-threatening prayers after going through some of the darkest times of my life. (I'll tell you more about that in chapter 3.)

Let me give you just one example of how God used one of the worst moments in my life to reveal Himself to me in a brand-new way. I was driving down the street on one of those days when it was beautiful and sunny, and everyone seemed to be smiling. All of a sudden I felt a sharp pain on my right side. It was like nothing I had ever experienced. I called my doctor, and she told me I may have pulled a muscle. Thinking I just needed to give it time to heal, I walked around feeling one sharp pain after another on my right side for several weeks. Yes, I said *weeks.* For weeks I walked around rubbing my side and asking people what organ was on that side of my body. People gave me a variety of diagnoses—I was told it was gas, a pulled muscle, and anything else they could think of. Finally I went to my mother and told her, "Mommy Bear, something is wrong."

Not even an hour later I collapsed in my father's arms in excruciating pain. Later I would find myself in the emergency room having a sonogram that revealed I had a gallstone the size of a tennis ball lodged between my rib cage and kidney. The technicians and nurses were astonished I had been walking around with that level of pain. I had to undergo surgery, and afterward I felt so good that I wanted to jump up and move around. The doctors and nurses couldn't believe I wasn't in more pain. I already knew God was a healer, but He used that situation to introduce Himself to me as *my* healer. He showed me that if I trust Him and surrender to His will, He will walk with me no matter how ugly the situation. I felt my body was betraying me, because it wasn't made to be sick and diseased. But if I had not gotten sick and been in so much pain, I would not have known God could give me the strength to get through it.

I can say without a doubt that dealing with betrayal has made me stronger. If it had not been for the friends who lied about me, I would not have been able to see who was for me and who was not, and knowing who is on your team is crucial to winning the ugly fights. Yes, it hurt when people falsely accused me, but their betrayal made me really seek after God. And I became a better person because the betrayal led me to search for the reason I was going through what I was experiencing.

Betrayal hurts, but I consider it a gift because it has taught me about God, life, others, and myself. If we truly learn the lessons of betrayal, those lessons can guide us into a purpose beyond our imagination. The hard part about betrayal is that it hurts, and everyone handles the pain differently. Some handle it by running away and not facing the lessons, and others wait to see what they can learn from the experience.

Betrayal could have made me bitter, but instead it taught me that people and situations come into our lives for a reason, and that reason isn't always roses and rainbows. The enemy only sends a Judas into our lives because we have a purpose that makes him nervous. He wants us to give up so we won't pursue our destiny. But one reason God allows us to struggle is the resistance makes us stronger. God will take us out of our comfort zone and put us in a position where we cannot lean on anyone or anything but Him so we will get stronger through the struggle. The ugly fights we go through can strengthen us if we change the way we look at them.

We have all dealt with betrayal in some way or form, but there is a gift and a lesson in everything we go through, both the good and the bad. The friends who betrayed me taught me that I needed to love myself more because I was letting them take advantage of me. I thought I would be very fertile and have lots of children, then my body betrayed me and I had to battle through infertility. I was angry and upset and wondered how this could happen to me. But that experience has given me the most beautiful gift: it showed me who I am and who I could be, and it led me to discover the joy of adoption.

Pain is part of your process to become ferocious, but how you choose to handle pain will determine whether it makes you bitter or better. I am better because I let betrayal teach me to believe what God said about me instead of what people said. I am better because I allowed betrayal to build me up and not break me down.

I know for a fact that changing the way I looked at betrayal helped make me ferocious. Your ugly fight may not be infertility. It may not be a health crisis or relationship drama, but it is something. Instead of running from the fight, ask what it can teach you. Ask God to show you how He wants to use it to bring you to something greater. I challenge you to look over your life, consider those who betrayed or hurt you, and instead of being bitter, allow yourself to see that pain as the start of something great in your life.

If you have faced the sting of betrayal and need to be healed, let me tell you, God is a healer. To help you become more ferocious in prayer, I have included a prayer much like the one I used when I needed to heal from betrayal. Use it to speak healing over your life, and expect God to bring blessing out of your pain.

PRAYER FOR HEALING FROM HURT AND BETRAYAL

God, thank You for loving me. Thank You for holding me when I couldn't hold myself. God, thank You for never leaving me lonely. God, thank You for not leaving me when others did. Thank You for never letting go of me.

God, thank You for giving me the capacity to love others even if they persecute me.

God, I confess that I have let people hurt me even when You told me and showed me who they were. God, I confess that I ignored red flags. God, I confess that I tried to control my life and not to give You full reign. God, I confess that I tried to handle things that You told me to release to You. God, I confess that I thought I was smarter than You. God, I confess that I rejected You and then got upset when I was rejected by man. God, I confess that I didn't always heed Your voice, telling myself it wasn't You. God, I confess that I ignored You so I could rebel and do what I wanted to do.

But, God, I thank You for redemption. I thank You for always holding me up. I thank You for purifying my mind, body, and spirit to do what You would have me to do. I thank You for removing people from my life before, and even after, they betrayed me. Thank You for giving me peace about broken relationships. Thank You for giving me joy in sorrow. God, thank You for Your kindness toward me. Thank You for protecting me. Thank You for salvation and for discipline. And thank You for keeping me.

God, I ask that You help me to forgive those who betrayed me. God, I ask that You help me to walk away from things that are not encouraging me to become the best version of myself. God, I ask that You help me to take You seriously. God, I ask that You reignite in me a deep honor and respect for You. Uproot everything in me that isn't like You, and cause me to bear good fruit.

I pray, God, that You open up doors of favor for every betrayal. I pray, God, that You direct me to my purpose and help me stay the course. I decree and declare that I am not who I used to be. I decree and declare that I am a threat to the enemy. I decree and declare that my faith is ferocious. I decree and declare that everything I touch is blessed and not broken. I decree and declare that I am the head and not the tail. I decree and declare that I am above and not beneath. I decree and declare that I am worthy of love and peace. I decree and declare that I am more than a conqueror.

I decree and declare that You are my leader, Lord Jesus, and I follow Your instruction. I decree and declare that I am lovely and marvelous in Your eyes. I decree and declare that I will walk as You have called to me to walk. I bind, rebuke, and destroy every curse and problem that keeps me from loving people in the way Your Word has called me to love them. I pray, Lord God, that You teach me to be selfless. Teach me how to walk in discernment and to exercise it with wisdom. Lord, help me not to stay in relationships that I know are not going to benefit me. I thank You for all these things. It is so by faith, and by faith so it is. Amen.

Speak Life

Create in me a pure heart, O God, and renew a steadfast spirit within me.

—Psalm 51:10

Betrayal doesn't have to make me bitter; it can prepare me for better.

God is creating in me a pure heart and giving me a steadfast spirit.

CHAPTER 3

Press Your Way Through

WANTED TO AVOID the pain of this story. I would love to skip over this part of my journey and just tell you about adopting my son Jason, but if I were to do that, I would be glossing over one of my most devastating fights. Every warrior has to learn to persevere even in the midst of pain, and this fight taught me how to pray in the midst of depression, loss, and true heartbreak. Even as I write this, I am attempting to hold back the tears.

Josiah Jackson was my first son. He was the first baby boy I would love beyond words. After my initial IVF cycle and Amauri's adoption, my husband and I decided to keep growing our family through foster care. At the time, we were looking for a baby boy. I can still remember receiving the email about JoJo. He had just been born, and his mother had several children, so his caseworker was sure we would be able to adopt him.

We were all beaming with excitement when I brought him home. After adopting Amauri when she was three, I finally had a little baby. We began to bond with Josiah as our son. I loved JoJo with all my heart and so did my church and my family. We were watching him grow and develop when I received an email that delivered the worst news I had ever received.

JoJo's caseworker said his biological life-giver wanted him to be placed with a different family. I felt as if my heart were being ripped out of my chest. I gave him his first bath and his first tummy time, and I was the only mother he had known. I cuddled him when he cried and fed him when he was hungry. I prayed for him and covered him spiritually. I was born to be a mother and to love people from a hurting place to a healed place. Yet here I was in more pain than I ever could have imagined.

We always have our plan, and then God has His plan. Well, in my plan JoJo was supposed to stay with us. He was supposed to be my first son and to be beside Amauri to greet the biological children God had promised me upon their arrival into the world. We anointed JoJo and prayed that he could stay with us, but the situation didn't change. Within twenty-four hours his caseworker would be coming to rip him from my arms.

His mother was well within her legal rights, so I shouldn't have been mad at her, but I was. I shouldn't have been mad at the lawyer and the caseworker, but I was. I had never felt so much sorrow and anger at one time.

I anointed his clothes as I packed them up, and then I went to my parents' house to meet the caseworker. I knew I would need my family's support when they came to take my JoJo. While we waited for the caseworker, I held JoJo and just kept praying. I knew I couldn't pray to keep him, because God never told me he was mine. I know when God tells me something is mine, but God didn't tell me I was to keep JoJo. So instead of praying for a way to keep JoJo in our family, as I wanted to, I prayed that God would cover and protect him wherever he ended up. I couldn't pray what I wanted; I had to pray what he needed.

Oftentimes we want to pray what we want, but part of being

ferocious is being willing to sacrifice. You have to set your desires to the side and allow yourself to pray for God's will instead of your desires: "not my will, but yours be done" (Luke 22:42). My heart wanted to pray for me, but I couldn't let that block me from praying the way God was leading me to pray for JoJo and his well-being.

After what felt like forever, the car came through the gate. His caseworker got out and approached me. It was clear her heart was saddened because she knew how much we loved and cared for JoJo. She literally apologized for having to take him. That is something else I want you to recognize—sometimes things are taken from you not because you are not qualified to keep them but simply because the journey for those things includes something you cannot give or because a bigger blessing is on its way for you.

I was qualified to love JoJo and would have loved him forever, but the plan God had for him outweighed my desire. So I handed him over.

His tiny hands and big, brown eyes seemed to be begging for me to take him back. My heart screamed, "Please don't take him!" My spirit screamed, "Please don't take him!" My whole body screamed, "Please don't take him!" But God said, "Let him go."

Everything in you may want to hold on to some things, but God says let them go.

PRAYING BY FAITH

I went into a deep, dark depression after losing JoJo. I was not angry at God, but I was discouraged in God. I felt like He was punishing me, when in reality He was pruning me. Gardeners cut back certain parts of a plant to encourage it to grow. That is what God was doing with me. He was cutting away parts that were keeping me from becoming the best version of myself to prepare me for something greater. According to my plan, losing JoJo was an absolute disaster, but God's plan was still to prosper me and not to harm me. (See Jeremiah 29:11.)

Every day for a year the pain of losing JoJo rang in my heart until God used it to heal my heart. Yes, you read that correctly. God used the hurt in my heart to heal me. In my brokenness I looked for scriptures such as Psalm 147:3, "He heals the broken-hearted, and binds up their wounds," and I would force myself to believe and pray what God's Word said was true.

During that season, the Word of God came alive in me, and it changed the way I saw myself, my situation, and my future. As I prayed God's Word back to Him, I saw the manifestation of what I prayed, as long as I believed what the Word said. And that is how I pray to this day. I pray on the level of my faith. I let God's Word dictate what I believe, and I challenge the enemy with the Word.

If you aren't careful, the enemy will try to make you believe you aren't worthy of receiving blessings. Through the failed rounds of IVF and losing JoJo, I was able to see that just because God allows us to lose something does not mean we will never experience anything better. God always has a plan. I couldn't see what God would bring after this heartbreak. I just believed He would bring something good, and I believed that because I believe the Word of God. The Bible is living truth, and if we will walk in the truth of what God has spoken, we will be able to step into new levels in life.

A WOMAN WITH AN ISSUE

A ferocious life of prayer and faith is often built in the midst of heartbreak. I learned the power of prayer while facing the pressure of a disabling pain. Even though we had JoJo for only two months, the pain lasted for years. Some people thought I shouldn't be in so much pain since he was with us for only a short time, but pain is an individual experience. Yet whether your pain has lasted for a long time or a short time, God wants to heal your hurt.

In an earlier chapter I mentioned the woman with the issue of blood who pressed through the crowd to get to Jesus. (See Matthew 9:20–22; Mark 5:25–34; and Luke 8:43–48.) She had been bleeding for twelve long years, seeing doctor after doctor to no avail.

The customs of that time forbid her family from being near her because, according to the Law of Moses, her bleeding made her unclean. Not only was she unclean, but anything she sat or slept on and anyone she touched would also be unclean. (See Leviticus 15:19–30.) Can you imagine how lonely and ostracized she must have felt?

She had been legally unclean for twelve long years, and for all that time, she had been living away from friends and family, unable to receive a hug or even a touch. If you have ever felt broken, if you have ever lost hope, you can relate to the woman with the issue. The woman was broken in body and soul, and Jesus was her only hope. So, believing that if she could just touch the hem of His garment, she would be made whole, the woman— weak after bleeding for so many years—pressed her way through the crowd, maybe even on her hands and knees, to get to Jesus. And she was in fact made whole.

The woman received the healing she needed after taking a life-changing walk of faith, and that is how I got through the bleeding of my heart after losing JoJo. I walked by faith. I knew I didn't want to stay where I was. I didn't want to be bitter; I wanted to be better. I didn't want to be angry; I wanted to have peace. I wanted to be a better mother to the daughter God had given me. And I still wanted to fulfill God's plan for my life and become the best version of myself. So I started taking intentional steps to become who I desired to be. I continued to pray God's Word over my life until hope sprang forth and I began to walk toward my purpose.

There are three powerful aspects of what the woman with the issue of blood did to find wholeness after so many years of bleeding: she had a heart to be healed, she knew what to reach for, and she had faith. Those are the same three things that helped me heal emotionally and spiritually after losing JoJo. They are how I found renewed strength in God to become ferocious.

She had a heart to be healed.

The woman with the issue of blood had gone to doctor after doctor looking for answers, and when they couldn't help, she pressed her way through throngs of people to get to Jesus. This tells me she had a heart to be healed. She was so motivated to be healed that she pushed past the obstacles—the rules of her culture and even the press of the crowd—to get to the One who could make her whole.

You cannot be healed if you won't pursue healing. I couldn't be healed from the pain of losing JoJo until I was willing to pursue healing. I had to be willing to talk about my problems and share my hurt and anger with God. Even before that I had to be willing to admit I needed healing, both in my heart and in my relationship with God. I had become so angry that it was beginning to consume me. But I wanted to be whole, so in the midst of my anger and pain I walked toward the healer and reached out to Him by faith, believing He would make me whole.

She knew what to reach for.

As the woman with the issue took those careful steps toward Jesus, the Bible says she told herself, "If I just touch the hem of His garment, I know I will be made whole." (See Matthew 9:21.) Some people think she was expressing her desire to touch whatever part of Jesus she could reach in the midst of such a throng.

But I don't think that was what was happening. I think the woman knew exactly what she was reaching for and why. Let me explain what I mean.

The garment Jesus wore was known as a tallit, often called a prayer shawl today, and it had tassels on each of its four corners called tzitzit. The tzitzit represented the commandments God had given the Jewish people through Moses, so they served as a constant reminder of the Word of God. When the woman extended her hand to touch Jesus, she wasn't just reaching for His garment; she was reaching for the power of His Word. And she didn't just let her fingers graze Jesus' garment. The Greek word translated "touch" in Matthew 9:21 is *haptomai*, which means "to fasten one's self to, adhere to, cling to."[1] The woman fastened herself to Jesus. She clung to His Word.

When my heart was broken after losing JoJo, by faith I reached for the Word of God and clung to His promises to me. I reached for the support of family and friends I'd had my whole life. I reached for testimonies of people who had overcome the same kind of pain. I reached for prayer and declared God's Word back to Him. There is nothing wrong with "Help me, Jesus," but there is power in praying specifically and strategically over a situation. There is power in finding scriptures that relate to our circumstances and reminding God of His Word. We can reach for the Lord, knowing we can "approach God's throne of grace with confidence, so that we may receive mercy and find grace to help us in our time of need" (Heb. 4:16).

She had faith.

When the woman reached for the hem of Jesus' garment, she was reaching for the promises in God's Word, but there was more to it. She was exercising faith in His Word. In the last book in the Old Testament, Malachi prophesied that "the Sun of Righteousness shall arise with healing in His wings" (Mal. 4:2,

NKJV). The word translated "wings" in that verse is a reference to the tzitzit.

The woman with the issue of blood touched the hem of Jesus' garment because she believed He was the promised Messiah who would have healing in His wings. She believed touching Jesus would make her whole because she believed He was who the Word said He was and that He could do what His Word said He could do.

As I mentioned previously, we pray on the level of our faith. We reach for God on the level of our faith. We grow spiritually on the level of our faith. And as we discussed in chapter 1, you cannot become ferocious in prayer or in life without faith.

When I was a child, my prayers were based on the fact that Jesus loved me, because I had sung "Jesus Loves Me" countless times and had faith that Jesus loved me. As I grew, I began to learn that Jesus was my healer and the Holy Spirit was my comforter; I learned that God was my provider and nothing was too hard for Him. As my faith matured, my confidence in who God was and what He wanted to do in my life showed in my prayers. When I was seeking healing, I reminded myself of God's Word. Second Timothy 1:7 says, "For God has not given us a spirit of fear, but of power and of love and of a sound mind" (NKJV), and Proverbs 17:22 says, "A merry heart does good, like medicine" (NKJV), so I declared that I had a sound mind and a merry heart, and the more I declared the truth over myself, the stronger I became.

At first all I could do was speak over my heart: "I am going to be OK. I will overcome this." Then I began to read and highlight scriptures that supported what I was saying to myself, such as 1 John 5:4: "For everyone born of God overcomes the world. This is the victory that has overcome the world, even our faith." The more scriptures I read, trusted, and believed, the stronger my faith became. And the stronger my faith became, the more my prayer life developed.

My question to you is, What are you doing to grow your faith? None of us, including me, can afford to remain in kindergarten forever. There are people to influence for God and souls to bring into the kingdom, but we need real street cred to win unbelievers to Christ. They have seen the fake and phony, and now it is time to let them see what a ferocious warrior looks like. Show them your scars by being vulnerable. Be authentic. It wasn't easy going through such a private ordeal in a public manner, but now everyone knows I am an overcomer. Today I want the world to know the devil is a liar and I have the faith to prove it.

It hurt my heart when JoJo was taken from us, but the healing process God took me through helped make me ferocious. I thought losing JoJo was going to destroy me. I thought the depression and pain would be the end of me, but instead it brought out strength in me I never knew I had.

Everything I thought was sent to break me and make me weaker made me stronger. Losing JoJo taught me that I could handle another IVF cycle even if it brought more disappointment. It taught me to pray what God says no matter how I feel. And it taught me to trust God even when I have to hand over what I thought was one of my greatest blessings.

I have never been arrested, but I have watched enough TV to know that when the police tell you to put up your hands, you should surrender right away and not put up a fight. When God told me to let JoJo go, I had to completely surrender to His plan. I walked away from JoJo without putting up a fight because I knew that was what God was calling me to do. I had to release JoJo and trust that God's plan for him was better than my own, and when I did, God healed me of my selfish pride and desire to take control.

It may be a natural reaction for us to want to follow our own plan, but it isn't wise. Remember what happened to Jonah. God called him to go to Nineveh, and Jonah tried to run from God by boarding a ship bound for Tarshish. So God sent a storm that would have wrecked the ship if Jonah hadn't insisted the crew toss him overboard. Jonah ended up in the belly of a great fish, where he spent three days before God had the creature vomit him onto dry land.

Jonah was willing to say yes to God after that, but he could have avoided a lot of heartache if he had just surrendered to God's will the first time. I sometimes wonder why Jonah tried to run in the first place. God is omnipresent, meaning He is everywhere, so there was no place Jonah could go where God wouldn't find him. The same is true of you and me. We might as well say yes and surrender to God the first time He speaks, because we cannot hide from Him and He knows what is best for us.

WHAT KIND OF WARRIOR ARE YOU?

You are in charge of how you respond to the fights you face in life. So what kind of warrior will you be? Some people are lazy warriors who always run away from the fight. Because they are afraid to face their fears, they remain stagnant in life and never move forward. They are too lazy to leap, too afraid to take on responsibility. Being a warrior is a big responsibility, and you cannot be lazy and win the fight. You have to choose faith over fear.

Or you could be the kind of warrior who plays the victim. We will talk more about this in chapter 10, but for now let me say this is my least favorite kind of warrior, and they rarely experience victory. These warriors always fight from the position of being a victim. They believe they never did anything to warrant what is going on in their lives and their problems are always someone else's fault. I also call these types of warriors "avoiders" because they avoid any kind of fight that requires them to take responsibility and face the consequences of their actions.

You can also be a tired warrior in a season when you feel as if you are losing everything and you just need a win. You keep on fighting, but you are tired. These warriors are neither good nor bad, but they lack the ability to see God in the things happening in the fight. So instead of growing in strength, they become weary. I could have become a tired warrior after losing JoJo, but I asked God to give me the strength to press through to find healing, and because He did, my life has never been the same.

Then there are the prideful warriors. These warriors face the fight without even considering God as their guide. They take on the fight without wisdom, and they think they are the only ones who can save anyone and the only one who can save themselves. They are reckless because they would rather fight without counsel than seek wise counsel.

We also have the naive warriors. These warriors don't guard themselves at all. They trust everyone and do not use discernment. Naive warriors are also easily deceived and detoured by the tricks of the enemy. They end up going through the same fight over and over again because they trust the people who take advantage of them for personal gain. They are drawn into unhealthy relationships with people who hurt them. They lose because of their gullibility, not because they lack power. They are simply too naive to see the devices of the enemy.

I could go on about the different types of warriors, but from this point forward I don't want you to claim to be any type of warrior other than the ferocious warrior. Ferocious warriors don't fear the fight. They learn the strategy of the enemy and willingly run into battle to take back everything the enemy tried to steal from them.

Ferocious warriors are a threat to the enemy because the enemy cannot control them. Ferocious warriors believe and trust God so much that they are not intimidated by the enemy. They have set their minds on obtaining the blessings and promises of God.

Ferocious warriors are diligent warriors, always training to become better than they were before. They take initiative and change the game. They are calculated warriors and have no problem working hard.

Ferocious warriors will go through the fire, the flood, the pain, and the sorrow of the fight to become better for the next battle. They approach the fight knowing God has the victory. Ferocious warriors don't mind being uncomfortable because they understand that sometimes God will give you something you are uncomfortable with just to train you for what is coming.

That is what happened to me. Had I never known what it was like to lose JoJo, I don't think I would have known how much I could endure. But in losing JoJo, I discovered the warrior in me. I discovered the strength that comes from putting my trust in God. I discovered a level of freedom I had never known. And I drew closer to God as I looked to Him and His Word for answers.

Having my heart broken opened it up to whatever God wanted to do. And God chose to bring Jason into our lives. Even after I lost JoJo, I never lost faith that I would one day have a son. I believe being able to release JoJo to God prepared me to receive the son He would later give me in Jason, but I will get into that in the next chapter.

I have said it before, but it bears repeating: God uses pain to help make us ferocious. The hard times help us learn to lean on Him and His Word, and they test our endurance. As we close out this chapter, I want to leave you with a prayer much like the ones I used when I needed God to heal my heart. Pray it over your life and trust God to use this pain to make you ferocious.

PRAYER FOR HURTING HEARTS

Lord God, I thank You for being my healer. I ask that You heal my heart. I confess, God, that I have not always loved You or Your people the way I should. I confess that I have sometimes been selfish. I confess that sometimes I have played the victim when You have called me victorious. So I thank You for not keeping a record of my wrongs and for forgiving me and cleaning me up when I make mistakes.

I pray, God, that You wash me clean of every hurt and pain that has caused me to rest in depression and not destiny. Receive my broken heart and make it brand new.

I ask, O God, that You strengthen me. Remove every dark spirit of depression, discouragement, and suicide from my heart, mind, body, and spirit. I ask You, Lord God, to open my eyes to see who I really am and who You are in my life. I ask, O God, that You would stir up the gifts inside me that I may be successful in the spaces You have appointed me to be successful in. I denounce and destroy every spirit that desires to keep me bound and broken, and I ask You to fill me up until I want no more. God, I ask You to bring meaning to every mess in my life and reveal Your glory in me.

God, place a hedge of protection around me. I decree and declare my heart is healed and whole, and I am not broken any longer. I decree and declare that my life is filled with peace, power, and prosperity. Thank You, God, for being my waymaker and my help in the time of trouble. I look to You for help in the midst of my trouble. I thank You for giving me another chance to seek Your face and for turning this situation around. I believe it is so by faith and by faith so it is. Amen.

Speak Life

He heals the brokenhearted and binds up their wounds.
—Psalm 147:3

God has a good plan for me, and He will heal my heart.

CHAPTER 4

Be Still

N O, THIS CANNOT be happening!" Life had been going so perfectly. Then like a thief in the night everything began to change, and I found myself in one of the ugliest fights I had faced so far. When I was a teenager, a fight like this one would have seemed like the end of the world, and I would have done all I could to defend myself and try to prove I was right. But I have learned that sometimes the best way to fight is to just be still.

When I was growing up and dreamed of becoming a mother one day, I knew there would be times when I would have to fight for my children. I just never imagined it would involve judges and Child Protective Services. I never thought I would have to go to court and face accusations from people who were like family to me. But the fight to become a mother has required all of that and more.

I once thought adoption would be an easy process, but after standing before judges and talking to lawyers, I can tell you it was the furthest thing from easy. Walking in the fullness of being a mother has taken a lot of paperwork, some hurt, and even the dismantling of close friendships. Adopting our son Jason was a hard, ugly fight, and the worst part is that I didn't see it coming.

THE UGLIEST FIGHT OF MY LIFE

Sometimes your fight comes out of nowhere and you don't know what you are supposed to do. That is what happened to me. As you know, after I lost Josiah, I went into a very dark place. I was so hurt that I didn't think I would recover. But through prayer, fasting, and learning to accept what God allows, by the time we were presented with the possibility of adopting Jason, I was open to the idea of adding another child to our family.

We were blessed to have Jason placed in our lives from birth. To this day we are so grateful for the gift his biological mother gave us. Amauri came into our lives when she was three years old, but we got to raise Jason from the time he was born. We were there for his first bath, his first steps, his first words—the whole nine yards. Then about a year after Jason was born, his birth mother relinquished her parental rights to Brandon and me, which brought us even more joy because we were that much closer to making things official. But that journey—oh my goodness, it was so long, and the process was excruciating.

Brandon and I had been raising Jason for about a year after the relinquishment and were ready to start finalizing the adoption when it seemed all hell broke loose. Instead of the adoption going smoothly, it was contested, and we had to face a judge to defend our character and prove we were not only ready to adopt but also that we were the best parents for Jason.

We faced the fight of our lives for almost two years. And the prospect of losing another son, this time after raising him for years, was absolutely petrifying.

I had never been in a courtroom for myself, but that's where I found myself, facing accusations that seemed to come out of nowhere. Worse, many of those accusations were made by people I once considered friends.

Because my accusers knew me so well, they used my struggle

to have biological children against me. I had to stand in court and talk about my battle with PCOS and the trauma of dealing with infertility. I had to suffer through having my character questioned by people who had known me for years. I felt denied and betrayed by individuals who had been like sisters to me.

I remember taking a deep breath and asking God how I could possibly endure so much pain from people I thought genuinely loved and supported me. It was a life-changing and life-breaking time for me because I had to choose whether to let the world know my story by going before the court to fight for my son, or to hide and act like Jason wasn't worth it.

It seemed crazy to have to go through so much resistance to finalize what we thought had already been established. But Brandon and I decided that if, after all those years, we had to fight in court for Jason to finally be ours, we would fight with everything we had. This wasn't like with Josiah. I knew God gave Jason to me, just as He gave me Amauri—I knew it from the moment I saw his face. So if I had to stand before a judge to fight for what I knew God said was mine, I didn't mind. We would not lose another son, especially since we had raised Jason all his life. I would be a ferocious mama bear.

During that ordeal it would have been easy for me to make myself a victim of circumstance. I had already lost so much to infertility; I could have just given up. Instead I looked at Jason and decided I would stand and I would fight. That meant I had to be transparent with the judges, jury, caseworkers, Child Protective Services workers, and lawyers because standing in the truth was the only way I was going to win this battle.

Trials are going to come into our lives. The enemy will come to accuse because that's what he does. He is an accuser of the brethren (Rev. 12:10), and the only way you can win when the enemy accuses you is by standing in the truth—the whole truth and nothing but the truth, so help you God. Sometimes that truth can hurt; it can expose and even humiliate you. But the truth, no matter how bad it is, will always set you free (John 8:32).

My family and the people who watched us raise Jason for so many years all came together and stood with us. They were our cloud of witnesses. They had watched our victories and our losses, they had seen us in our light and in our dark, and they were able to remind us that God had seen us through in the past and He would do it again.

I wish I could get into the full details of the case to finalize Jason's adoption, but that would take away from the joy of who he is and the healing he brought, not just to me but to my entire family. Yes, the court battle was hard, but God gave us the victory. On September 15, 2018, we adopted our son in front of all of our family and friends, and it was a day we will never forget. I feel like with adoption, the judge, instead of a doctor, is the one who gets to deliver the baby. What was so great for us was the judge who was with us through all the court battles was the one who finalized our son's adoption and officially delivered Jason to us.

Having Jason Gabriel, whose name means healing and strength, become a permanent member of our family helped me heal physically and emotionally after all the pain and disappointment I experienced with the failed rounds of IVF, losing JoJo, and then losing some longtime friendships during the court battle. Jason was the medicine our hearts needed. Being able to take him home as a Coleman and to never worry about him being taken away brings tears to my eyes even now. It was the hardest fight I have faced so far, but I would do it all over again and wouldn't change a thing.

LET IT GO

When I was taken into court, I had to give custody to God. I couldn't fight with a tit-for-tat mentally. I couldn't go back and forth with my accusers. I had to be silent and let truth fight for me. I had to stand still and hold my peace while letting God fight my battle, and I had to admit that it was time to let some friends go.

When I was younger, I didn't realize some of the people in our lives won't be able to go with us where God is taking us. That does not mean we cannot help them along the way, but we have to stop being angry when someone doesn't have the capacity to love us or support us as we move toward where we desire to go in life. It's better to move on without them than to limit ourselves to what they can handle and thereby forfeit what God wants to do in our lives.

I've had to let go of some friendships to find healing and strength and to become the person God was calling me to be. The people in your life have been placed there to teach you something and help you grow and develop, but not everyone will be there for a lifetime.

Oftentimes we need more from a relationship than it has the capacity to give us. As a result we either give up on the relationship or we give too much and end up being taken advantage of. It is easy to lose yourself in a relationship when you're trying to be something you're not.

Healthy, nurturing relationships encourage you to face your obstacles, tests, and trials head-on without fear. If we stay attached to relationships that don't have the capacity to feed us, we will become accustomed to not being truly fulfilled.

I'm telling you this because I had to take responsibility for the role I played in allowing various friendships to become unhealthy. I allowed people to use me, lie to me, mistreat me, abuse me, and then throw me away, and I have to take responsibility for that. I am thankful both for the experiences that helped me and the ones that hurt me because they revealed who was for me and who was not.

God has a way of using the worst fights of your life to show you who is in your corner. During the adoption process and through my failed IVF cycles, I watched my relationships with close friends deteriorate before my eyes. I felt betrayed by their testimony in and out of court, and it broke my heart.

At one time I had a group of girls who were like sisters to me, and I watched God change the number from several to a few. We grew up together, and we had been there for one another through some of the most joyful and painful times of our lives. But again, not every relationship is meant to last a lifetime.

In that season, I came to realize some of the people I thought were friends were like tares in my life. In case you're not familiar with the term *tare,* let me explain what I mean. In Matthew 13 Jesus shared a parable about wheat and tares, which are also called weeds in many Bible translations. Jesus said:

> The kingdom of heaven is like a man who sowed good seed in his field; but while men slept, his enemy came and sowed tares among the wheat and went his way. But when the grain had sprouted and produced a crop, then the tares also appeared. So the servants of the owner came and said to him, "Sir, did you not sow good seed in your field? How then does it have tares?" He said to them, "An enemy has done this." The servants said to him, "Do you want us then to go and gather them up?" But he said, "No, lest while you gather up the tares you also uproot the wheat with them. Let both grow together until the harvest, and at the time of harvest I will say to the reapers, 'First gather together the tares and bind them in bundles to burn them, but gather the wheat into my barn.'"
>
> —MATTHEW 13:24–30, NKJV

Because the wheat and the tares looked so similar, the farmer knew he couldn't just rip up the weeds. He had to let them grow up together, and when they were fully developed, he would separate the two. The tares would be burned, and the wheat would be prepared for harvest.

After a point I began to feel like the wheat in the parable, like I was being choked by fake friends who were trying to appear real. I had to learn that when God has called you to a higher place, you can't take everyone with you. Just because you grow with someone during one season of your life does not mean you will always be able to grow with that person.

I should be clear that sometimes the people (or things) you have to pluck from your life are not bad, but their removal is necessary both for your growth and theirs. Sometimes God will separate you from someone because that person is depending too much on you and not on God. Or you may need to sever the relationship to grow into a better version of yourself.

I have always been someone who wanted to help everyone, even if it killed me in the process, so releasing unhealthy things in my life has been one of my greatest challenges so far. During the time we were fighting for custody of Jason, I had several unhealthy and outright contaminating relationships in my life, and God wanted me to separate myself. But for the longest time I couldn't bring myself to do that, so I ended up getting burned by so-called friends.

If your friendships are helping you grow and walk in God's will for your life, then you have healthy relationships. When a relationship becomes one-sided and the other person is always concerned about what you can do for him or her, it is unhealthy and you need to let it go.

One major reason we lose ugly fights is because we don't want to admit our part in letting the wrong people get close to us. I used to let people take advantage of me because I'd become comfortable in dysfunctional friendships and was trying to fix everything and everyone. The truth is I was looking to be accepted by everyone. So when we went out, I paid for everything. When someone asked me to do something, I jumped to respond to whoever was calling. I told myself I was being helpful, and I was being helpful. But the truth is I was feeding my need to be needed and control everything. I had been taken advantage of and used so often that I could not identify when someone truly loved me and when someone did not. Because of that mindset, I held on to people and things that I should have let go.

I couldn't let God be God in my life until I was able to release the dysfunction and walk in nothing but the truth—the truth that I was more than enough. The truth that I didn't have to pay for friendship. The truth that people who love me are going to love me no matter what. The truth that I am not perfect and cannot fix everything no matter how hard I try. I had to walk in the truth that I couldn't be my friends' savior, even if it cost me the friendships.

STAND STILL

When I was facing my battles in court, I came to a place where instead of trying to fight to prove I was right and the accusers around me were wrong, I chose to stand still, hold my peace, and let the Lord fight the battle. That's right. Sometimes the way to fight is to just be still.

In Exodus 14, when God was bringing His people out of slavery in Egypt, Moses told the Israelites, "Do not be afraid. Stand still, and see the salvation of the LORD, which He will accomplish for you today. For the Egyptians whom you see today, you shall see again no more forever. The LORD will fight for you, and you shall hold your peace" (vv. 13–14, NKJV).

When Moses spoke those words, the people of Israel were in an impossible situation. The Red Sea was in front of them, and Pharaoh's army was pursuing them from behind. The Israelites didn't know what they were going to do. In fact, they began to complain that God had led them out of Egypt to die in the wilderness.

The truth is God had led them to that precise place but not so He could leave them to die. The Bible says:

> Then the LORD said to Moses: "Tell the Israelites to turn back and encamp near Pi Hahiroth, between Migdol and the sea. They are to encamp by the sea, directly opposite Baal Zephon. Pharaoh will think, 'The Israelites are wandering around the land in confusion, hemmed in by the desert.' And I will harden Pharaoh's heart, and he will pursue them. But I will gain glory for myself through Pharaoh and all his army, and the Egyptians will know that I am the LORD."
>
> —EXODUS 14:1–4

The whole situation was a setup. God wanted to show Pharaoh how powerful He was, but more than that, He wanted the people of Israel to see He was greater than their enemies, greater than their obstacles, and that no matter how big the problem, He could lead them to victory.

You probably know the rest of the story. God parted the Red Sea so the Israelites could walk across on dry land. Then, after the people of God made it across, He caused the waters to return and drown the army of the Egyptians. God didn't just deliver His people; He destroyed their enemy in the process. And the Israelites didn't even pick up a sword.

When I was in court facing accusations from people who knew me, I had to stand still. That doesn't mean I didn't pray. That doesn't mean I didn't prepare for court. That doesn't mean I didn't follow the lawyers' and judge's instructions. It means I gave God control of the situation and the outcome. It means I had faith in His Word and refused to doubt what He had spoken to me about Jason. It means I got quiet, listened for God's instructions, and obeyed His voice, believing He would do in the situation what I couldn't accomplish myself.

When we are faced with an ugly fight, it's natural to want to do *something*. But sometimes we just need to be still. I have come to understand that sometimes the fighting isn't about your swing but about your ability to stand in the face of the thing that scares you and trust that God will be with you no matter what. Your ferocious attitude in some battles is about your surrender to God's ferocious power at work in you. The power God has given us to fight the good fight of faith doesn't always require us to do something. Sometimes we just need to stand still and see the salvation of the Lord.

This reminds me of a game I used to play. When I was a little girl, my siblings and I loved to play hide-and-seek, but we liked to play at night so it would be dark. We would gather in a common area, explain the rules, and pass out flashlights because this wasn't ordinary hide-and-seek—it was blackout hide-and-seek. If you thought you heard or saw someone, you could flash your light, but if you didn't hear or see anything, you couldn't use your light. You had to search for things and hide in the dark.

We could play this game for hours. There were a lot of places you could hide in my parents' house. But one of the best places, if you had time to get there, was in the linen cabinet behind the towels and blankets. It was a great spot because it was small, and it covered the person hiding. At the time I was small enough to fit into that space. Now, not so much. My knees alone would keep me from getting back into those cabinets (LOL).

No one could see you in the linen cabinet, but they could hear you, so you had to be extremely still. No matter where you were hiding, to win the game, you couldn't move, talk, or even breathe loud because if you did, whoever was it would find you. But if you were able to be still, the person looking for you would eventually give up because you were so hard to find.

What does a children's game have to do with your situation? Plenty. You may be in a dark circumstance and think you don't know what you are supposed to do; if you will find a place and get still, God will give you what you need. There is a reason Psalm 46:10 says, "Be still, *and know that I am God*" (emphasis added). Being still is just part of the equation. We get still so we can focus on God and His strength instead of our weakness.

Just as God had a plan for the people of Israel when they were hemmed in at the Red Sea, He has a plan for you. He sees what you are facing, and He will bring you through it.

It reminds me of the song "Surrounded (Fight My Battles)." Throughout the battles in court I realized I was never standing alone. The power of God was surrounding me, and it is surrounding you. "As the mountains surround Jerusalem, so the LORD surrounds his people both now and forevermore" (Ps. 125:2). Whether or not you feel God in the midst of the fight, you are never in the battle alone. As soon as you realize God is surrounding you, the enemy won't stand a chance.

When we fought for Jason in court, we trusted that God was surrounding our family, and He guided us through what to do and placed people in our lives to help us win the fight. That's another sign that God is with you—when He sends you support to help you fight the battle.

I didn't have to physically fight or hurt anyone. I felt like fighting that way, but God told me to be still and surrender, and He helped us every step of the way. God brought the victory. I just had to be willing to separate myself from certain relationships so

I could truly grow up into who God wanted me to be. Once I was able to stop trying to save friendships only God could save, I was able to truly focus on God and connect with Him in a deeper way. When we lack the ability to give God control of things, we sometimes end up delaying our growth, or someone else's, because we are trying to hold on instead of truly letting God take care of the situation.

No one likes going through pain and sorrow, but it is so worth it once you realize how your faith and prayer life are developed in the ugly fights. I would not have become the most beneficial, impactful, and confident version of myself if I had never been hurt and broken. Being broken caused me to become a better mother because it drew me closer to my family; a better daughter because it showed me how to appreciate parenting; a better sister because it showed me who really had my back; and a better friend because after losing some of who I thought were my closest friends, I was able to see what true friendship was.

I am grateful for what the fight for my children taught me, but more importantly I am grateful for what it gave me. I don't think I could love Amauri and Jason more if I had given birth to them myself. Losing Josiah helped prepare me for what was coming. Josiah was the first son I got to love. Jason is the first son I get to raise, and the fight to keep him helped me to figure things out about myself, my friendships, and the power in letting go even when it hurts.

Every ugly fight has been a small gift from God that revealed the true nature of those around me and allowed me to see who was for me and who was not. The fight to adopt Jason aided in my healing from being a people pleaser and ultimately helped me to walk in freedom and be an example of faith and hope for those I minister to.

Had I never gone through the court process for adoption, I

would not have learned how to trust God with something that was completely out of my control and in the hands of people who didn't know me or my relationship with Jason. I had to learn to trust our lawyers and the judge. They were a type of God (the judge) and Jesus (the lawyer) for me. I had to stand beside them and trust that at the end of the day we would finally walk away with the legal proof of what God had already established for us in heaven. And we did.

CHOOSE VICTORY

Sometimes the enemy tries to use what you have been through to suppress you. Don't let what you have been through make you a victim. Let the friends who left you, the divorce, the rape, the molestation, the insufficient funds, the pain of where you have been make you a survivor. The enemy wants me to be a victim of the things in my life that bring infertility, such as anger and depression, but I refuse to let infertility bind me up. I refuse to let infertility define me. I choose to be productive in my life. My fertility isn't just about what I can birth but also about what I can build for God's kingdom.

I have decided to stop being a victim and to stay rooted in the Word of God. I could have continued in sadness and accepted the label put on me, but I chose to get free in my mind through prayer and worship. I chose to stop being provoked by people who didn't want me to be successful, and I surrounded myself with successful and inspirational people. I chose to consistently be myself and hope people who were consistent would find me.

I have found that a ferocious prayer life isn't formed during the beautiful times in life; rather, it is built in the barren and broken places you think God can't turn into something beautiful. Through the trials I have faced, in and out of court, I learned how to pray not only for myself—so I could stay loving and compassionate and open with people—but also for those who persecuted, accused, and made judgments about me. And I learned to lay aside my flesh that made me comfortable in dysfunctional relationships and let go of the things that were hurting me.

Through the adoption process the enemy tried to take my heart for people and for friends who were like sisters to me. But eventually I realized what I was going through was really an answer to prayers I had prayed years before. I had prayed for God to separate me from the things that weren't like Him. It may have taken time, but He answered.

Almost losing Jason made me ferocious in prayer, and my hope is that your dark situation will make you ferocious too. God has the ability to turn your whole life around, but it starts with you. In my book *Faithing It* I closed each chapter with a prayer for the reader, but to be ferocious, you must learn how to pray for yourself. That is what my fights taught me. They taught me the importance of looking into the mirror and being able to intercede for myself. That is the power of this book. I don't just pray for you; I show you how to ferociously pray for yourself.

The following prayer is adapted from the one I prayed during my court battles. Use it to declare victory in your circumstances. It is time to get ferocious.

PRAYER FOR VICTORY IN YOUR CIRCUMSTANCES

God, You are a lawyer in the courtroom and a righteous judge. You hold all power and victory in Your hand. Thank You for being the fighter of my battles.

God, I confess that I have been inattentive to Your voice and have pursued my own will instead of Your will for my life. God, I confess that I have hurt people in my own hurt. I confess that I have not always done what pleases You, but I thank You that You are my kinsman-redeemer.

I thank You for forgiving me and for making my crooked paths straight.

God, I thank You that Your blood covers a multitude of my sins. I thank You that You are truth and that You are my light. I thank You that You keep those who cry out to You close. I pray, God, that You work things out according to the will You have already spoken. I give You custody of my life and my family. I give You custody of my mindset. I give You custody of this court called life. I trust that You are the judge, and Your judgment will go forth no matter what, so give me the strength to handle that judgment.

God, I know that You are my peace, so I ask that You bring me peace in the midst of the case. God, I pray that You protect my kids from the arrows that surround us. I pray that You increase my faith that I may be protected from the attacks of the enemy. I pray, God, that You confuse my enemies and that no weapon they form against me will prosper. I pray, God, that You reveal what I need to get the victory in this circumstance. I pray, God, that You cover me in the blood of Jesus and protect me from the accuser of the brethren. I pray, God, that Your love would consume me and my family in the midst of this fight. Surround me with a cloud of witnesses. Help me that I may be able to help others.

I denounce every evil friendship attached to me and my life. I denounce the agenda, tactics, and accusations of the enemy over my life. I denounce the authority of the enemy over my home and over my life, in the name of Jesus. I declare that healing will take place in my mind, heart, spirit, and soul in the name of Jesus. I pray that every tongue that rises against me You will indeed condemn.

I pray that You give me favor for the fight, including financial favor. I pray that You lift me out of the snares of the enemy. I thank You, God, for I know the victory belongs to Jesus, and that is the victory I decree and declare over my life in the name of Jesus.

I thank You, God, that You will expose every lie and redeem me with truth. God, sharpen my discernment so I will know who is for me and who is not. Help me to forgive those who have broken my heart. Give me the ability to stand in victory without worrying about those who have hurt me because of their own pain. Do not allow me to fall prey to the hands of the enemy. It is so by faith, and by faith so it is. Amen.

Speak Life

Then you will know the truth, and the truth will set you free.

—JOHN 8:32

God is my judge, and Jesus holds my victory.

I walk by truth, and the truth will set me free.

CHAPTER 5

Free to Be Ferocious

WHAT WAS THAT?" I knew something happened in my spirit because I suddenly felt a freedom unlike anything I had ever known. After two failed IVF cycles, I had fallen into a deep sadness and was feeling lost and scattered in thought. So I called a wonderful woman, who is now my spiritual mother, just to talk and pray with her. On that phone call she prayed yokes off me I didn't know were there. The depression and discouragement that were trying to overwhelm my heart and mind were broken off my life, and I began to live in a level of success and purpose I otherwise would never have known.

What I experienced that day was deliverance. When I was growing up in church, *deliverance* meant being set free from a demonic presence that was oppressing a person in some way. But a mentor of mine opened my eyes to another way of understanding *deliverance*. She defined it as a process of releasing things—weights, addictions, unhealthy relationships—that are keeping you from moving to your next level. Deliverance is something everyone needs. It is how we move from one place in life to the next. It is how we are revived. Restoration and peace come when we are able to walk in deliverance. Deliverance isn't spooky. It is about acknowledging that there is something you need to release and then having the drive to seek freedom.

Sometimes we shy away from deliverance because of pride. We don't want to admit we are struggling with certain things. But Proverbs 16:18 says, "Pride goes before destruction." I was able to move closer to my destiny because I was open to deliverance. If I had let pride convince me to keep quiet and not reach out to God, I would never have been able to move forward in life. If you aren't careful, pride will trick you into thinking you are moving forward when you are really just standing still.

Deliverance is part of becoming a ferocious warrior because it brings healing and spiritual growth. It is how we overcome the weaknesses of our flesh and the mindsets that keep us from pursuing God's plans and purposes for our lives and the earth. It clears away all the "stuff" so we can draw closer to God and truly understand our power and authority in Him. Most importantly it gives us the clarity to recognize the tactics of the enemy and the strength to fight back.

It is much harder to win a battle when you are weighed down by burdens and locked in chains. That is why deliverance is so important. It sets us free to be ferocious.

If you don't choose to walk through deliverance and let God heal you from the inside out, you will remain weighed down by dark things. If you truly love God and want to be ferocious, then you must do what it takes to break free from pain, sorrow, anguish, and anything else weighing you down so you can fight from a place of liberty.

Everything I have faced in life has taught me something new about myself and about growing in God. The principles I learned about getting free and staying free have made me a better, stronger, more ferocious person. So in this chapter I want to share what I call the D principles that have helped me break free of bondage, maintain my freedom, and grow in God.

DELIVERANCE PRECEDES PROGRESS

The first D is *deliverance*. We all need deliverance at one time or another. We all have hindrances in our lives that keep us from walking in the fullness of power God has given us. Whether it is a compulsion, a bad habit, or a cycle we continually repeat, we all have areas in our lives where we need God to bring wholeness and freedom.

I believe most people know when they need deliverance. They may not know the precise problem they are dealing with, but they know when something isn't right. They know when there is something in their lives that is not like God. Fear, depression, hopelessness, and defeat may be common in our world, but they don't have to be part of the life of a believer. So if your thoughts toward yourself or others are often dark or you feel as if you are carrying heavy burdens, it's time to seek deliverance. If you are always jealous of what other people have, if you are using food or shopping or relationships to fill a void, or if you are just feeling stuck, there is probably something going on inside of you that you need God to deal with.

God wants you to be free.

Galatians 5:1 says, "It is for freedom that Christ has set us free." You never have to wonder whether God wants to set you free. Jesus described deliverance as "the children's bread" in Matthew 15:22–26. It belongs to us as children of God.[1]

Bread is something that sustains us, and the things that give us sustenance help make us strong. God wants us to tap into the power of deliverance so we can stay strong in Him. When we don't give our bodies proper sustenance, we become weak and unhealthy.[2] In the same way, if we allow ungodly habits to remain in our lives, we will become weak and vulnerable to attacks from the enemy. But when we seek God for deliverance, we will gain health, strength, and renewed life.

The enemy preys on our weaknesses. He will use anything he can to influence our lives and thwart our destiny. To close doors the enemy would use to get us off the path to our purpose, we must consistently go before God and ask Him to reveal anything in us that is not like Him. God wants us to be filled with more and more of Him so we can be ferocious and manifest His power on the earth. The more we rid our hearts and minds of things that are not like Him, the more room we will have for Him.

Deliverance requires humility.

Deliverance requires humility because before you can be set free, you must acknowledge that there is a problem and you need God to help you. That help may come as you look in the mirror and pray over yourself one of the many ferocious prayers in this book. Or it may come as you stand in a room full of prayer warriors who call out everything dark in your life.

However deliverance takes place, it requires you to remove yourself from a place of pride and humble yourself before God. His power will grow in you the more you surrender your position of power and give Him control of your life. I've heard it said that in God the way up is down. You cannot avoid humbling yourself if you want to be free to become ferocious and move to the next level in your walk with God.

Often people experience deliverance after receiving prayer from a pastor, prophet, or apostle in the church. That is what happened to me. A phone call with my spiritual mother broke chains off my life, and those chains remain broken to this day. Even if it's not a pastor, we all need people in our lives who can touch and agree with us and even cover us in prayer. We need ferocious warriors who have ferocious faith and ferocious prayer lives.

When God reveals something you need to release from your

life, it can be helpful to have someone stand in agreement with you for your deliverance. Look for someone who is spiritually mature, perhaps one of the intercessors on the prayer team at your church or someone with experience in deliverance ministry. I believe if you ask God, He will lead you to someone who can pray with you. But you can also pray for yourself.

In the Sermon on the Mount, Jesus said that instead of judging others, we should first cast out the beam in our own eye so we can see clearly.[3] (See Luke 6:42, KJV.) The word translated "cast out" in that verse means to eject, drive out, pluck, expel, or send away.[4] This tells me that whether I need to be delivered from a bad habit, wrong thinking, or some kind of demonic oppression, I can pray for ungodly influences to be removed from my life and expect to be set free. I can confess God's Word over myself and expect it to root out the things that are not like Him.

In Matthew 18:18 Jesus said, "Whatever you bind on earth will be bound in heaven, and whatever you loose on earth will be loosed in heaven." We have authority to bind the works of the enemy and demand that he cease and desist wreaking havoc in our lives.

Yet as we walk in this authority, we must seek God for wisdom and discernment. Not every problem is caused by a demon that needs to be cast out. Sometimes we need to develop new habits. You may not have a spirit of lack; you may just lack the discipline to save money. Sometimes we need to let go of the friends who hold us back when God is telling us to move forward. Sometimes we need to forgive. We must ask God to reveal what has us bound and what we need to release. If we don't, we may destroy something that we just needed to put in its proper place. There is nothing wrong with social media, for instance, but if it consumes you, it is not in its proper place, and God may call you to release it for a season to refocus on Him.

If we do not seek the wisdom of God, it is possible to sever relationships that only needed to be pruned, or to cut something out of our lives that was not really the problem at all. Sometimes the fear of love can make us push people away who can help us grow. Sometimes we cut people out of our lives because of a disagreement when learning to better communicate could have fixed the problem. Always seek the wisdom of God to know where the real problem lies and what you need to let go, knowing that the Word promises, "If any of you lacks wisdom, you should ask God, who gives generously to all without finding fault, and it will be given to you" (Jas. 1:5).

Deliverance is progressive.

Sometimes God will bring immediate breakthrough, but more often deliverance happens progressively. As you release the pain from yesterday and acknowledge your choices today, you can expect a better tomorrow. But you have to start moving in a new direction to avoid repeating the same unproductive patterns. When we have done something one way for a long time, change can be difficult. Even if we did not like the results we were getting in the past, doing things differently can feel "wrong." That is how the enemy can get us to fall back into old patterns.

True freedom is possible, but it can take time. It can take time to get to the core issue and discover the real you buried underneath all the facades you've been wearing. It can take time to face yourself and the things that have caused you pain. But becoming the best version of yourself requires that you address areas of wounding and weakness over time. Your life may not change after one prayer session, but as you keep going before the Lord, He will pull back the layers and help you deal with every issue keeping you bound.

This is why we need spiritual parents. Spiritual growth and healing take time, and a spiritual parent can help support you through the stages of your journey. Spiritual parents are different from mentors. A mentor is a teacher who helps guide you; a parent nurtures you. When I was drowning in discouragement, God sent someone into my life who not only prayed for me to be delivered but also kept walking with me so I would make the choices that would help me stay free and continue to grow. She has become a spiritual mother to me, and she has helped me grow through consistent care. Much like natural parents, spiritual mothers and fathers are consistent; they don't come in and out of your life on a whim. They walk with you through your journey to wholeness.

Just as it is with anyone else you allow to get close to you and speak into your life, you must be careful about who you choose to be a spiritual parent and what you receive from that person. I have found that a good spiritual mother is a fountain of wisdom; she is compassionate, caring, and consistently growing herself. She allows you to have access to her and is always there as you grow in your developing relationship. God brought a spiritual mother into my life to pray for and nurture me. It wasn't something I prayed for, but if you ask God to bring someone into your life to walk with you as you journey to freedom, He will lead you to the right person.

Whether you have a pastor or spiritual parent pray for you, or you pray for yourself, deliverance is just the first step. Once you have received deliverance, you must maintain your freedom, and you do that through the next D principle: *discipline.*

DISCIPLINE BRINGS LASTING FREEDOM

When my sister and I were just a little younger, she was very skinny. And I, well, I have never been super skinny, but after the rounds of IVF my weight really went up. We wanted to try something called the lemonade challenge to lose weight. It wasn't the healthiest way to lose weight, but it sounded relatively simple, so we decided to try it. In reality, it wasn't easy at all. The challenge consisted of drinking a very nasty concoction of salt water, and then a mixture of water, lemon, and cayenne pepper for a week. It would take a lot of discipline, but we knew we could not expect to lose weight if we were not disciplined enough to follow through. So we started the program, and, well, let's just say Sarah lasted way longer than I did. I got a taste of that saltwater flush, and that was all she wrote. I could not—would not—do it. It required too much from me or, at least, more than I was willing to give at the time.

I admit, the lemonade challenge required a higher-than-normal level of discipline. But have you ever needed to do something to make yourself better, and you had what you needed but struggled to be disciplined and follow through? I have been there, as I started diet after diet and tried to work out. Even now I have to discipline myself to love myself no matter where I am physically. I had to learn that loving myself could not be contingent on my being skinny, because if that never happened, I would be signing myself up for depression. I also had to learn to love myself enough to work on my spiritual discipline in the hopes that it would spill over into my natural discipline.

Deliverance is like your spiritual diet. It is your opportunity to shed the weight of pain and depression off your life. However, deliverance that is not followed with discipline will not last. Life is filled with opportunities for you to strengthen your character, and discipline is necessary to develop a strong character. The Word tells us that discipline "produces a harvest of righteousness and peace for those who have been trained by it" (Heb. 12:11). Some people confuse discipline with consistency, but they are not the same. In order to be consistent in your life, you are going to need discipline.

Discipline is important after deliverance because it will help you stay focused on the things of God. We can get delivered, but to maintain our freedom and forward movement, we must discipline ourselves to read the Word, worship, pray, and show compassion. Developing discipline after deliverance will keep you in alignment with the will and ways of God and help prevent you from returning to old habits and reclaiming the baggage you were freed from.

Discipline can be defined as "training that corrects, molds, or perfects the mental faculties or moral character."[5] It is the practice of training people to obey rules or a code of behavior. When you get delivered, you should demonstrate new behavior. You do that by training your heart and mind to fall in line with the Word of God.

Some people are intimidated by the word *discipline.* But there is no lasting freedom without discipline. Proverbs 25:28 says, "Like a city whose walls are broken through is a person who lacks self-control." Cities whose walls are broken through are vulnerable to attack, and a person without discipline is vulnerable to falling back into bondage. To maintain your deliverance, you must discipline your thoughts (Phil. 4:8), desires (Ps. 37:4), and words (Jas. 1:26). You can grow in self-control by studying God's Word daily, praying earnestly to maintain your freedom, and asking the Lord to keep you alert to the ways the enemy might seek to put you in bondage.

Also make it a point to fellowship with others who are seeking to become disciplined in their walk with God. You don't want to have relationships with people who bring out the worst in you. Keep people around you who are going to hold you accountable to being who God has called you to be, people who won't allow you to revert back to who you were before God delivered you. If you don't have those kinds of people in your life, ask God to send you the proper support. He will help you.

Discipline is not just a matter of following strict rules and keeping a bunch of dos and don'ts. It is a way we model the next D principle, our *dedication* to God and our growth.

DEDICATION MOTIVATES

Dedication is how you deepen your relationships with God and others, and it is how you become a ferocious warrior. The word *dedicated* means to be "devoted to a cause, ideal, or purpose" or "given over to a particular purpose."[6] This has always been the mark of a warrior. Think about the many warriors in history; most of them accomplished great feats because of their dedication to a cause.

What are you dedicated to? What is your purpose for wanting to be ferocious? Are you tired of being tossed and turned in life? Are you tired of the enemy taking authority over your life? If so, are you willing to dedicate yourself fully to God so you can walk in His power and dismantle the works of the enemy?

When we dedicate ourselves to God, we give ourselves over to Him. We don't live to satisfy ourselves or to fit into someone's idea of who we should be. We live to please the Lord. In Psalm 16:8 David painted a picture of dedication when he wrote, "I keep my eyes always on the LORD. With him at my right hand, I will not be shaken." If we keep our eyes on the Lord, they won't be on our problems, our weakness, or our pain. They will be on the One who makes us ferocious, and we will not be shaken.

Whether we realize it or not, we all are dedicated to something, and sometimes we are dedicated to things we should release. Sometimes we are dedicated to things that are not tied to our ultimate purpose. Some of us are dedicated to being broken, victims, angry, depressed, lost, confused, bitter, and people pleasers.

You may not be ferocious in life and in prayer because you aren't dedicated to the right things.

Change what you are dedicated to and you will see things change in your life. I have known people who were dedicated to thinking and speaking negatively about themselves. Of course they didn't see it that way. They thought they were speaking the truth, but their "truth" was based on the enemy's view of them, not God's perspective.

So often we allow negative things and people to change how we function in life. I have heard people pray but not really believe what they were saying was true for themselves. Dedicate yourself to God and align what you believe about yourself with what He says is true. (See appendix A.) Affirm yourself with God's Word every day, and things will get better. If you love yourself as God loves you, your prayer life will show it. When you really allow God to guide you, things begin to change for you.

DRIVE DIRECTS YOUR COURSE

The last D principle is *drive*. We are all driven by something. Some people are driven by fear, others by ambition, and others by guilt and regret. It is important that you take inventory of your heart because whatever drives you determines where you end up.

One definition of *drive* is "to operate the mechanism and controls and direct the course of."[7] Think about your life. What drives you? What drives you to pray? What drives you to grow? Who or what are you letting control and direct your course?

Are you letting your friends drive you? If so, be careful. If the friends around you are not driving you to be the best version of yourself, you are sure to wreck. You cannot develop if you surround yourself with people who are not interested in growing.

If you truly want to be ferocious, give God the wheel and let Him direct your course. Let His love for you and the promises in

His Word drive you to be ferocious against the enemy. If He takes the wheel, He will lead you to victory.

There is freedom in surrendering to God and not trying to fight your battles on your own. There is power in letting God lead you as you face the ugly fights. Job 11:13–15 says, "Surrender your heart to God, turn to him in prayer, and give up your sins—even those you do in secret. Then you won't be ashamed; *you will be confident and fearless*" (CEV, emphasis added). If you want to be confident and ferocious in the face of life's storms, surrender to God.

When you hear the word *drive*, you may also think of driving a car. When you drive, you put your hands on the wheel and keep an eye on your surroundings as you move toward your intended destination. This is how I approach prayer. I surrender myself to God, asking Him to direct my prayers, and I stay alert to what is going on around me to guard against the attacks of the enemy. That is also what you must do to grow in God and be ferocious: you must give God control, stay cognizant of the people surrounding you, and keep your eyes on Him.

No one can help you the way God can when you make deliverance, discipline, dedication, and drive a regular part of your life. Becoming ferocious is a progressive process, and you grow more ferocious as you let God use each test and trial to pull anything out of you that is stunting your growth and replace it with more of His Spirit and character.

As I said before, every fight I have gone through has taught me something new about myself, about God, and about what it means to be a ferocious warrior. I never want to just tell people what I have gone through; I always want to share what I learned and gained from the fight. Through the ugly fights I've endured, I have learned principles that have helped me persevere in prayer, grow more consistent in my walk with God, and become ferocious.

In the next chapter we will look at how to think like a warrior so you can prevail in the midst of the battle. But before we continue, use the following prayer to ask God to use the power of deliverance, discipline, dedication, and drive to help you grow strong in Him and become ferocious.

PRAYER TO IGNITE DELIVERANCE, DISCIPLINE, DEDICATION, AND DRIVE

Father God, I thank You for loving me enough to want me to reach new levels. You knew me before I was in my mother's womb, and You are dedicated to bringing out the best in me. I want to be better than I am right now. Help me to be who Your Word says I can be. Help me to seek You for deliverance. Don't let pride keep me from getting free from everything that holds me back from the life You called and created me to live. Let me develop the discipline to maintain that deliverance, and give me dedication and drive to become ferocious in prayer and in life.

Lord, remove all pride, anger, bitterness, depression, and anything else that keeps me stagnant and unsuccessful. Lift me out of the barren places and help me to bring forth fruit that remains. Lord, give me a new perspective that allows me to excel in life. Reveal methods and strategies that will help me grow stronger and more ferocious in my faith.

Help me to become more aware of the devices of the enemy. Help me to always acknowledge You. Help me to be aligned with Your will and Your Word. Lord, help me to hope in You when I face fierce battles in life and things don't seem to be going well. Help me remember that You cause all things to work together for my good.

Show me who You have called me to be in this season. Let me see myself the way You see me. Give me supernatural favor and joy. Deliver me from yokes and bondage that have weighed me down. Give me a passion to follow You. It is so, and so it is. Amen.

Speak Life

Trust in the LORD, and do good; dwell in the land and befriend faithfulness. Delight yourself in the LORD, and he will give you the desires of your heart. Commit your way to the LORD; trust in him, and he will act. He will bring forth your righteousness as the light, and your justice as the noonday. Be still before the LORD and wait patiently for him; fret not yourself over the one who prospers in his way, over the man who carries out evil devices!

—PSALM 37:3–7, ESV

I am delivered from my past, disciplined for my future, dedicated to the right things, and driven to become the best version of myself. I will trust in the Lord, and as I delight myself in Him, He will give me the desires of my heart. I submit my way to Him, and He brings forth my righteousness.

CHAPTER 6

Think Like a Warrior

I HAD TO LEARN how to live in the limelight, in the heat of scrutiny, at a very young age. I was just seven years old the first time someone asked me for an autograph. It was so different to be noticed in that way. It is strange to grow up with possibly just as many people who hate you as there are who love you. You see people get close to you just to take advantage of who you are or, even worse for me and my siblings, to take advantage of who our parents are, specifically my giant of a father.

After you have been hurt and betrayed so many times, you learn to build a defense mechanism against people. As children, my siblings and I were always trying to figure out who was for us and who was against us. We always had to be in the mindset of a warrior because we never knew when we would find ourselves in conflict with people who prematurely judged us or made us feel inadequate or superior as "Jakes kids."

Thinking like a warrior for us was not about being mean or unapproachable. Thinking like a warrior was about making sure we knew when the fight was necessary. It took time, but I learned that things that will help you grow or develop are worth fighting for, but a fight that will take more from you than it will give is unnecessary.

We often spend our lives fighting battles that are not helping us grow and then wonder why we haven't made any progress. The reality is that we lack the necessary discernment to know what to fight for, so we keep people in our lives whom we should let go of. We fear being hurt, so we build walls around ourselves to keep people out, not realizing that we lock ourselves inside those walls along with our pain, hurt, anger, bitterness, resentment, and regret. The only thing our mind can focus on when we build those walls is the hurt and pain behind them. If our mindset is always fixed on our failures and people who reject us, we will never win the battles we face every day.

A DISCIPLINED MIND

When I first started writing this book, I watched several TV shows and movies about gladiators. I figured, Who better to teach us about being ferocious than those who fought for their very survival, with or without armor, winner take all? Like gladiators, ferocious warriors are fighting for their lives. They are relentless in prayer because they know it is the only thing that assures their survival.

Because the stakes are so high, gladiators do not just rush into a fight; they go into battle only after rigorous training. And they do not win fight after fight simply because of the skills they develop; they win because they know how to discipline their minds.

When I was a little girl, I was very shy and quiet and had trouble figuring out where I fit. I spent a lot of time trying to force myself to be what I believed people wanted me to be instead of walking in who I truly was. I used to pad my bras to look like I was developing. I would wear contacts, trying to look like the "cool kids." I had no fashion sense, by the way. I didn't pick that up until I was about twenty-five years old. I had trouble with my confidence until I saw women similar to me walking with their heads up and loving the skin they were in.

It encouraged me to change my mindset and how I viewed myself. I learned that being confident in who I am does not make me less humble. I learned that my confidence needs to be in who God made me to be. Now as an adult, mother, wife, and pastor, I can truly say I know who I am, and the devil can't tell me anything. I don't just embody the character of a warrior; I embody the mindset of a warrior.

You would be surprised how much your thinking controls your outcomes. The Bible tells us, "For as he thinketh in his heart, so is he" (Prov. 23:7, KJV). This lets us know that how we think has the power to change what we experience in life. Almost everyone I have mentored or counseled got truly free only when the person was willing and able to change his or her mind. When you are able to think like a warrior, you are able to win like a warrior.

You are responsible for the story you tell yourself and what it produces. If you want to produce things that are beneficial, then you have to watch your mind. Yes, you read that correctly. We have often been told that we should watch our mouths, but I want to encourage you to also watch your mind. Watch what you think about yourself and what you let yourself believe. (See appendix A.)

Romans 12:2 says, "Do not conform to the pattern of this world, but be transformed by the renewing of your mind. Then you will be able to test and approve what God's will is—his good, pleasing and perfect will." In order to truly be in the perfect will of God in this fight of faith, you have to consistently be transformed by the renewing of your mind, and the only true way to renew your mind is through God's Word. The more you study the Word and believe the Word, the more your mind will change.

That is what happened to me. I began to study the Word in a translation that was easy for me to understand, and God used it to help me change my mind about myself. One day as I was looking outside, I began to marvel at the beauty in nature. As I looked at the trees, the birds, and the sky, the Lord reminded me of Genesis 1:27 and told me that as lovely as His creation is, it was not made in His image the way I was. When I realized God considered me a masterpiece, I knew I needed to start seeing myself that way too. The Word of God is a guide that helps us refocus and align our perspective with God's. When you are able to see your situation from God's point of view, you will be able to conquer things that were sent to destroy you.

Proverbs 3:5–6 tells us, "Trust in the LORD with all your heart and lean not on your own understanding; in all your ways submit to him, and he will make your paths straight." It is very easy to get caught up in pursuing your own desires and leaning on your own understanding. But sometimes your own understanding comes from a dark place and can begin to rot you from the inside out. Your understanding must be submitted to God, because if it's not, it will be out of alignment with His Word, and living out of alignment with God's Word will lead to your demise. This isn't an average fight. This is a spiritual war, and in order to win it, you must anchor your thoughts in God's Word and submit your understanding to Him.

WHAT ARE YOU THINKING?

One of the devices of the enemy is to plant negative thoughts in your head that detour you from what God told you in the beginning. That was actually the very first trick the enemy tried with mankind. The serpent convinced Eve to shift her faith and believe what he was saying over what God had commanded her and her husband. When the first woman, who had been made from Adam's rib, shifted her faith, she began to think differently. She began to think God was holding out on her and that she lacked something, even though she lived in paradise and was so close to

God that they literally took walks together every day. Yet because she began to think differently when she fell for the serpent's lies, she got her husband to think differently, and they ended up disobeying God and introducing sin into the world.

One thought in your head can change the trajectory of your life. To think like a warrior, you have to monitor both your thoughts and the people you let influence your mindset.

Have you let people tell you what to think? Have you let people tell you who you are? Sometimes you can be your own worst enemy because of the way you choose to think. If you aren't careful and you allow negative thoughts and concepts about yourself to penetrate, they can form a stronghold. That is an idea you think is true but is actually false.

The Bible tells us to "demolish arguments and every pretension that sets itself up against the knowledge of God, and...take captive every thought to make it obedient to Christ" (2 Cor. 10:5). You can demolish strongholds and change your mind by simply not allowing the things not aligned with truth to lock into your thoughts. We must remember our enemy is a master manipulator. Jesus said, "He is a liar and the father of lies" (John 8:44), and we defeat him with the truth. John 8:32 says, "You will know the truth, and the truth will set you free." Notice it's not just the truth that sets us free; *knowing* the truth brings liberty.

Don't let your situation create a stronghold in your mind. When you cannot find peace and joy, consider what you have allowed into your mind. Are you believing things about your situation or yourself that are not of God? If so, you may need to clear your mind by worshipping God and spending time in prayer. Or you may want to turn on some worship music or listen to an audio version of the Bible to change the atmosphere around you and reorient your thinking. It is clear from the Psalms that David often felt discouraged, but he encouraged himself in the Lord by praying, worshipping, and reminding himself of who God is. First Samuel 30:6 even tells us, "David was greatly distressed, for the people talked of stoning him.... But David *encouraged himself in the* Lord *his God*" (mev, emphasis added). David affirmed himself, and that is one of the things you will have to learn in order to truly be a great warrior. To be ferocious, you will have to know how to walk in a new affirmation that gives you new strength.

We can control our thoughts; we don't have to let them control us. Remember, 2 Corinthians 10:5 tells us to "take captive every thought to make it obedient to Christ." And Philippians 4:8 tells us, "Finally, brethren, whatsoever things are true, whatsoever things are honest, whatsoever things are just, whatsoever things are pure, whatsoever things are lovely, whatsoever things are of good report; if there be any virtue, and if there be any praise, think on these things" (kjv). Paul is telling us to focus our thoughts on the things that are attached to who God is. This is how we keep our thoughts in proper alignment. To think on things that are true is to think on the things of God, because He is truth.

I have learned, and am still learning, how important what I think is. I did not realize a lot of my life was dysfunctional just because of the way I was thinking. Now I tell my "crew boos" all the time that they should speak well and think well so they can produce well. Our thoughts are just as important as what we say. So if you are in the heat of a battle, my question to you is, What are you thinking? Are your thoughts in alignment with the things of God? Are you taking every thought captive to make it obedient to Christ?

We are empowered when we take control of our thoughts and what we allow ourselves to believe. What you believe about yourself, you ultimately become and project onto those connected to you. Have you ever made a decision you saw the effects of much later? That is the power held in our minds. One decision can shift your whole life.

If you plan to win against the enemy, you must think like a warrior. But that involves more than disciplining your thoughts and aligning your beliefs with God's Word. Because I love acronyms, for the remainder of this chapter I'm going to break down the word *warrior* to look at how ferocious warriors think to win the fight.

W—WEAPONS

To think like a warrior, you must know what weapons are at your disposal and how to skillfully use them to destroy whatever is in your way. When David was going to face Goliath, he didn't use the weapons everyone else was using in battle. Saul, the king of Israel, dressed David in his own coat of armor, put a bronze helmet on his head, and gave him a sword to use. But after trying to walk around in Saul's armor, David took it off because he wasn't used to the armor and sword and could not use them skillfully.

David had used a slingshot many times to defeat smaller obstacles. So rather than taking up unfamiliar weapons, David pulled out the weapon he had trained to use. First Samuel 17:40 says, "He took his staff in his hand, chose five smooth stones from the stream, put them in the pouch of his shepherd's bag and, with his sling in his hand, approached the Philistine."

With so many options available to him, David chose a slingshot to defeat Goliath because he knew how to use it to defeat his enemy. But "the weapons we fight with are not the weapons of the world. On the contrary, they have divine power to demolish strongholds" (2 Cor. 10:4). You have many weapons at your disposal: worship, prayer, reading the Word, fasting, and wisdom, just to name a few. The more you learn about what weapons are available to you and how and when to use them, the more ferocious you will be against the enemy. (We'll discuss a ferocious warrior's three most important weapons in chapter 7.)

A—APPROACH

How you approach your obstacle is as important as your weapon. First Samuel 17:48–49 says:

> As the Philistine moved closer to attack him, David ran quickly toward the battle line to meet him. Reaching into his bag and taking out a stone, he slung it and struck the Philistine on the forehead. The stone sank into his forehead, and he fell facedown on the ground.

When David faced Goliath, he did not run away in fear. He did not say, "I am not qualified for this fight." He did not say, "I am too young." He did not say, "I can't do this without help." The passage says David ran quickly toward Goliath to meet him at the battle line.

David determined he would meet his enemy head-on and take him down. David was so clear about his plan that he even told Goliath exactly what he was about to do. In 1 Samuel 17:45–47, after Goliath disrespected God yet again, David told the giant Philistine:

> You come against me with sword and spear and javelin, but I come against you in the name of the Lord Almighty, the God of the armies of Israel, whom you have defied. This day the Lord will deliver you into my hands, and I'll strike you down and cut off your head. This very day I will give the carcasses of the Philistine army to the birds and the wild animals, and the whole world will know that there is a God in Israel. All those gathered here will know that it is not by sword or spear that the Lord saves;

for the battle is the LORD's, and he will give all of you
into our hands.

When David faced Goliath, he made a point to shut him down.
That is how you approach the enemy. You don't face the enemy
with your doubts and fears; you approach him knowing you do
not have to be afraid because the battle is the Lord's.

Your approach is important because it will either give your
enemy the upper hand or surprise him. I don't believe Goliath
expected David to run at him, but David did run. David didn't
slowly take Goliath down; he ran toward him. He ran toward the
obstacle in his way, and that is the best way to fight—to approach
your obstacles without fear and even to run after them.

Don't back away from the fight. If you think your strategy isn't
working, change your approach. If you've been praying and there
has been no change, start fasting too. If you have been declaring
victory and the situation seems to be getting worse, begin to
decree God's Word. (See appendix B.) Change your approach, but
don't run away in fear. No one ever got the victory by walking in
fear. Approach the fight knowing the victory belongs to you.

R—REACTION

Your reaction as a warrior is very important. To react to hurt,
betrayal, or a bad doctor's report with dignity and grace takes
mental discipline. Ferocious warriors use wisdom. If you react to
situations emotionally, you will not be effective in battle. David
did not go after Goliath emotionally; he was strategic. When you
think like a warrior, you go into the battle with a clear head and
your strategy intact.

It is important that you do not allow your emotions to drive
you in a fight instead of using wisdom. If you aren't mindful
of your reaction and you respond emotionally instead of with
wisdom and the proper strategy, you could end up losing the fight.

As I said, your reaction is a mental exercise. You choose whether to control yourself in a situation. If you don't respond with a strong mind, your circumstance will not improve. It may even get worse. In the social media world there are a lot of trolls, and when you post things, you open up your page to scrutiny, both positive and negative. People can be really cruel; they can say mean things just to get under your skin, trying to break you because they are broken also. It took me a long time to stop fighting back and wanting to respond to every mean statement. I had to learn which battles to fight and which ones to ignore.

I always felt as if I needed to defend myself, but sometimes my response just made things worse. Either my words would be used against me, or I would end up wasting my time going back and forth with people. My mother always says silence can't be quoted, and my granny used to say if you don't want anybody to know something about you, don't write it down for everyone to see. Your reaction to obstacles, setbacks, or people who antagonize and torment you reveals how you think. So think like a warrior. Be confident in the knowledge that God is your defense (Ps. 59:9), and respond to your obstacles with wisdom after seeking God for the right strategy. And please remember, everything doesn't require a response.

R—REST

This topic is one of my favorites. So many of us get so worried and concerned about what is going on in our lives that we don't take time to rest. In Mark 4 Jesus and His disciples were in a boat on their way across the sea when they suddenly found themselves in the middle of a storm. The disciples were afraid, thinking they were going to die, and all the while Jesus was sleeping at the back of the boat. When the disciples woke Him, anxious because they thought they would drown, Jesus "got up, rebuked the wind and said to the waves, 'Quiet! Be still!' Then the wind died down and it was completely calm" (v. 39).

In this moment, Jesus showed us what we are to do when we are going through a storm, and that is rest. God does not want us to respond to situations with fear and worry. His Word says, "Cast all your anxiety on him because he cares for you" (1 Pet. 5:7). God wants us to cast our cares and burdens on Him because He cares for us.

Sometimes God will have us act in a situation, but sometimes He just wants us to rest. Hebrews 4:9–11 says:

> There remains, then, a Sabbath-rest for the people of God; for anyone who enters God's rest also rests from their works, just as God did from his. Let us, therefore, make every effort to enter that rest, so that no one will perish by following their example of disobedience.

The rest referenced in this passage is the Greek word *kata-pausis*, which can mean "calming of the winds." It also denotes "a putting to rest."[1] We rest in God by trusting Him instead of trying harder. As Bible teacher Joyce Meyer wrote, "When we try to do everything in our own strength and leave God out of the equation, we just get worn-out and frustrated by our mistakes and failures. But when we lean on God, we actually enter into His rest and can enjoy our lives, no matter what our circumstances may be."[2]

There are many ways to rest in God. We may rest by standing firm in faith and resisting the doubts and distractions from the enemy. We may rest by taking a few days away in order to fast, pray, and worship because that evokes God's presence. We may rest by choosing to sleep peacefully as we trust God to work things out.

We may also choose to sleep, not because we are weary but

because we are weeping. Psalm 30:5 says, "Weeping may endure for a night, but joy comes in the morning" (NKJV). Sometimes God needs you to rest so He can bring you joy in the morning. Thinking like a warrior is understanding when it is time to rest and when it is time to train. Even the best warriors don't fight 24/7. Everyone needs rest mentally, physically, and spiritually.

Part of being ferocious and a real threat to the enemy is knowing that you can rest in God and in the truth of His Word. God has it all under control, and the sooner you realize that, the happier you will be in life. When Adam and Eve were in the garden, they were at rest knowing God would supply their needs. God took care of them, and He will take care of you. Jesus said, "Do not worry about your life, what you will eat or drink; or about your body, what you will wear. Is not life more than food, and the body more than clothes? Look at the birds of the air; they do not sow or reap or store away in barns, and yet your heavenly Father feeds them. Are you not much more valuable than they?" (Matt. 6:25–26).

What are you resting in? Are you resting in your strength, your wisdom, your ability to respond to the enemy's attacks? Or are you resting in God? Worrying is worthless. As Moses declared in Exodus 14:14, "The Lord will fight for you; you need only to be still."

I—INNOVATION

To be a ferocious warrior, you need to be able to think differently. You need to be able to look at things that would have frightened you and instead see hope. You need to be able to look at a crisis and see an opportunity for God to reveal Himself in a brand-new way. Being open to divine innovation is what separates the victorious from the victims, because it causes you to see beyond what is to what could be.

Innovation is "the introduction of something new; a new idea, method, or device."[3] But it can also refer to changes made to something already established.[4] Raise your expectations and believe God for something greater in your life. He "is able to do immeasurably more than all we ask or imagine, according to his power that is at work within us" (Eph. 3:20).

Let God give you a vision for the future He has planned for you. Open your mind to new possibilities. And when God shows you how your life or situation can be, take steps forward to make it a reality. Your choices will determine your outcomes. You have the power to shape your future, for good or bad.

Just because something seems established does not mean you don't have the power to change it. One of my old mentors used to say the things you see are subject to change. You can change where you are if you are willing to believe God, who has given you the power to change it.

O—OBSERVATION

Warriors need to be observant. The Bible says, "Be alert and of sober mind. Your enemy the devil prowls around like a roaring lion looking for someone to devour" (1 Pet. 5:8). We must be watchful of our surroundings because the enemy is waiting for an opportunity to devour.

God wants to bring change, renewal, increase, healthy relationships, and much more, but the enemy prowls around looking for a way to stop what God wants to do in our lives. He wants to devour your purpose and keep you from becoming the best version of yourself by getting you to open yourself to the wrong people and the wrong beliefs and get out of alignment with God's plan for your life. Openness may seem like a good thing because we want to be open to what God wants to do in our lives, but opening our hearts and minds to the wrong things can leave us carrying burdens we were never meant to bear and fighting battles that are not ours to fight. Sometimes we open ourselves to things that damage us instead of encouraging change in us.

The enemy wants to find a way into your life, and he will use any opening available, so watch what you open yourself to. You should never be open to anything that does not change you for the better. Eve opened her ears to the serpent, and Adam opened his mind to a deceived Eve, and because of that mankind fell. It is important to be careful about what you open your mind, heart, and spirit to believe and receive. We sometimes open ourselves to things that please our flesh but do not do anything to strengthen our spirits; sometimes our choices leave us open to depression, bad habits, or addictions. All these things will give the enemy the opportunity he needs to walk in and devour what God wants to produce in your life.

It is important to know what tempts you to sin because that is what the enemy will use against you. The devil does not just tempt you with things that hurt you. He also tries to block you from your destiny by placing things in your face that look like what you want but are not what they seemed to be once you open them. Have you ever received a beautifully wrapped gift that you were waiting to open, and when you finally opened it, the gift wasn't something you wanted? That's like what the enemy does. He distracts us with something beautiful while he's setting us up for a fall.

Pay attention to what you watch, listen to, and accept as truth, because opening yourself up to the wrong things can leave you broken. Guard yourself with the Word of God. Great warriors always protect their hearts, minds, and bodies from unnecessary damage, distractions, or detours. Don't open yourself to things that please you but don't strengthen your faith. You wouldn't keep your front door open all day, and you shouldn't leave yourself open all the time either. The Bible tells us, "Above all else, guard your heart, for everything you do flows from it" (Prov. 4:23).

Be observant of who is surrounding you and ask God to reveal whether those people are in your life to grow you or tear you down. Be observant of how you spend your time. Warriors have a mission, so they are not supposed to take on every task and opportunity. The enemy will be satisfied keeping you busy doing good things if that means you are not pursuing God's purpose for your life. We often take on too many responsibilities and become overwhelmed. Sometimes a no is necessary to preserve your strength and keep yourself available for what God wants to do.

Be observant. Watch and pray. Don't leave yourself open to the enemy. When you are playing a basketball game or some other activity that involves catching something, being open is a good thing. But the only things we desire to be open to as ferocious warriors are things that lead to victory and reveal God's glory. As a warrior you need a mindset open to change and renewal, but you should not be open to everything. You are a force to be reckoned with, so be observant and pay attention to what you allow into your heart, mind, and spirit.

So we have the weapons of a warrior, the approach of a warrior, the reactions of a warrior, the rest of a warrior, the innovation of a warrior, and the observation of a warrior. But there is a final *R*.

R—REWARD

The reward of the warrior is the reason we all fight. It is what's on the other side of the battle. When I was watching those movies and TV programs about gladiators, most of the men and women were fighting for some type of freedom, and even now we fight for freedom. Knowing what you are fighting for will keep you motivated when the fighting gets fierce. It is what will help you keep charging when all hope seems lost. Knowing what you are fighting for gives you laser-sharp focus so you can fight strategically. You do not want to be someone who fights just for the sake of fighting. To fight strategically, you must know why you fight. Warriors are always thinking of the reward they will reap from the battle. The Word promises that God "rewards those who earnestly seek him" (Heb. 11:6).

There are many different ways to view rewards in your life. Sometimes we see the manifestation of our expectations as a reward, but when you really begin to look at your life, you can see the reward in many things. Your freedom is a reward. Peace, power, purpose, and prosperity are just a few of the rewards waiting at the end of your fight.

You may be fighting right now, but you are fighting from a place of victory. In Psalm 37 David wrote, "Commit your way to the LORD; trust in him and he will do this: he will make your righteous reward shine like the dawn, your vindication like the noonday sun" (vv. 5–6). One of the best things to take into a fight is the knowledge that you will win. Gladiators walk into a fight with confidence in their ability, knowing they can and believing they will win. I want you to know that when you think like a warrior, you don't think of defeat. You think of destiny. Your destiny is attached to the fact that you will win this fight.

There is a reward after all of the pain and sorrow you have been facing, and that reward is victory. The Book of Hebrews tells us that Moses "regarded disgrace for the sake of Christ as of greater value than the treasures of Egypt, because he was looking ahead to his reward" (11:26). Just as Moses did, you should look ahead to your reward. You should expect to win. Your thoughts should always land at "I will win." However it looks and whenever it comes, be encouraged in knowing that you will win. Think like a warrior and you'll win like a warrior.

Let the following prayer encourage you as you ask God to

give you the mindset of a warrior so you can experience ferocious victory.

PRAYER TO THINK LIKE A WARRIOR

Father God, I thank You for the power of my mind. I thank You for Your thoughts toward me. I thank You for the power to believe in myself and to believe in others. Lord, I pray You help me to change my mind if my thoughts are not aligned with Your will and Your way for my life. I pray that You strengthen me to be greater than I was the day before. Let my mind be on You and no one else.

Lord, help me to apply my mind to things that will benefit me and not break me. Help me to surrender and sacrifice every thought that makes me feel unworthy of the purpose You have for my life. Lord, I thank You for helping me have a mindset that helps me grow and become who You have called me to be. Let my intentions be right with You.

God, help me with my observation of others and my observation of myself. I come against any seeds of thoughts that have been planted in my life by the enemy. I refuse to give the enemy power over my mind. I submit my thoughts to You. I declare that according to Philippians 4:8, I will think on things that are true, noble, right, pure, lovely, admirable, praiseworthy, and excellent. I will not give the enemy a place in my mind. I give You full authority over my mind.

I ask, God, that You help me to identify and know what my weapons are and how to use them. Lord, help me to change my approach when needed and always to exercise wisdom. Help me not to be quick to react but quick to listen. Help me to be watchful.

Lord, I ask that You teach me how to rest but don't allow me to get tired while I am operating in the gifts and power You have given me. Lord, help me to know when it is time to strengthen my spirit and when it is time to rest in knowing that You have it all under control. I pray, God, that You cause me to walk in peace like never before. I pray, God, that You show me how to be open but also teach me how to guard my heart. Help me not to fight the wrong way but to think like a kingdom warrior.

I thank You, Lord, for training me. I thank You in advance for the rewards of victory, power, purpose, prosperity, and peace You have waiting for me. Thank You for being the light that directs my path. I give You glory and praise for being my waymaker. It is so, and so it is. Amen.

Speak Life

No, in all these things we are more than conquerors through him who loved us.

—ROMANS 8:37

I am a warrior. I will think like a warrior, and I will not give up. I am more than a conqueror through Him who loves me.

CHAPTER 7

The Weapons of a Warrior

"I F I PERISH, I perish" (Est. 4:16). Those are the famous words of a biblical queen who knew how it felt to go through hard times. Queen Esther, one of my favorite women in the Word of God, has such a remarkable story that there is a whole book in the Bible named after her.

Esther, whose birth name was Hadassah, lost her parents at a very early age and was raised by her cousin Mordecai. Though the Jewish people were living as captives in Persia, Mordecai taught Esther to walk in the things of God. Most importantly he taught her to fast and pray.

During the reign of King Xerxes, Esther became part of a group of women from whom Xerxes would select his next queen. The women went through an extensive, yearlong preparation process, and ultimately Esther was the one who found favor with the king. But becoming queen was not the end of her story. At some point after Esther married Xerxes, Mordecai discovered that Haman, one of the king's nobles, was plotting to kill the Jewish people.

There was only one way Esther could save her people, and that was to go before King Xerxes and plead for her life and her people. Up to that point, Esther had not told anyone she was Jewish because Mordecai instructed her not to, so she didn't know how the king would react. Plus the law said you had to be summoned to see the king, even if you were the queen. Anyone who approached Xerxes without being summoned would be killed unless the king extended his gold scepter to the person and spared his or her life.

Before presenting herself to Xerxes, Esther fasted for three days, and she asked all the Jewish people and her maids to fast with her. Then she went before the king. Not only did he extend his scepter to her, but he ultimately issued a new order that saved the Jewish people from annihilation and he then had Haman killed instead.

No one can avoid dark times in life, not even a queen. Darkness will either overcome you or you will overcome it, but it will not just go away. You cannot become a ferocious warrior if you run from the dark places in your life. Too many people expect to win the ugly fights without doing any work, but that is not the way we become victorious. The greatest warriors consistently study and train with their weapons.

I can remember the first time I ever went to a gun range. Before I went in to shoot, I had to choose my gun, my bullets, and a target because you can't shoot without them. I had my own space, which at first made me nervous because it seemed too open and not safe enough. After a while, though, I realized I didn't need to be nervous or scared because most of the people there were like me, trying things out for the first time.

But the real beauty of the experience was that everyone there had someone with them who knew how to handle the weapons. They were the experts who knew what to do, and they could teach us how to do it. I didn't have to worry about getting accidentally shot or moving my gun the wrong way because there was someone with me who knew how to handle guns. I felt safer knowing not only that I wasn't alone in my beginner experience but also that I wasn't only with beginners.

The people who knew how to work with the guns had been trained to do so. They practiced their craft and became very skilled at it. That is exactly how God wants you to be. You too have weapons that you need to train to use.

You cannot win a fight you are not willing to consistently train for. Sometimes God trains you to become better by taking you through some of the worst things you have experienced. But you can defeat whatever you are facing if you undergird yourself with the proper weapons.

When Esther faced a situation that could have cost her life, she used three weapons that should be in every ferocious warrior's arsenal: prayer, fasting, and God's Word. In this chapter I want to look at each one because they are our most powerful weapons against the enemy.

THE WEAPON OF PRAYER

When I was growing up, prayer did not seem very powerful to me. But as I got older, I began to realize that every time I got in trouble and began to pray, things started to shift in my life. Prayer is one of the most powerful weapons you can use against the enemy because it is how you bring the authority and power of God into your situation.

When Esther decided to risk her life to go before the king about Haman's plan, she immediately called a fast. In biblical times calling a fast was synonymous with seeking God in prayer. Esther knew she could not win the fight in her own strength and ability. Her beauty and history with the king were not going to win the day. She needed the power of God working in the situation, and she needed His favor on her life when she went to see the king.

Esther pulled out the weapon of prayer when the stakes were high, and many of us do the same thing. We seek God when our backs are against the wall and we can't figure a way out of the situation. But prayer is not just for special occasions. It is not just for circumstances that overwhelm us. Prayer should be a lifestyle.

Esther was no stranger to seeking God. After calling the fast and committing to go before the king, Esther said, "And if I perish, I perish" (Est. 4:16). That means her confidence wasn't in God working things out a certain way. She trusted God no matter what the outcome was. That shows her relationship with God wasn't shallow. She believed God for her safety and success, but she knew God was still faithful, even if He answered another way. That kind of confidence isn't built by attending one prayer meeting or making one trip to the prayer closet. It points to an intimacy with God developed over time.

Make prayer a lifestyle.

Prayer must be a lifestyle. In a letter to the Thessalonians, Paul wrote, "Pray continually" (1 Thess. 5:17). In a letter to another group of believers he wrote, "Do not be anxious about anything, but in every situation, by prayer and petition, with thanksgiving, present your requests to God" (Phil. 4:6). Communicating with God should be something you do every day to sharpen your spiritual walk and deepen your connection to God. Prayer doesn't just cover and protect you; it shapes your environment, your personality, and your responses to life's obstacles. Prayer sharpens your discernment so you don't waste time on unproductive relationships. Prayer is how you keep God in the center of whatever is going on in your life, and it is how you invite Him to intervene in the situation.

The enemy expects you to reach for God when things are going wrong and to neglect prayer when things are going right. So when you start making prayer your lifestyle—something you do whether things in your life are going great or absolutely horrible—you surprise the enemy. The enemy thinks you are going to let discouragement outweigh your desire to get to your destiny, but he cannot overwhelm and oppress you unless you allow him to.

Pray and prepare.

If you don't have a consistent lifestyle of communication with God, you won't be able to handle the weight of the responsibility that comes with what you are seeking in prayer. Every new level in life brings a heavier weight of responsibility, whether spiritually or in the natural, and you must pray and prepare for what you desire God to bring into your life.

I have two fantastic dogs now, a cocker spaniel and a little Yorkie. My cocker spaniel has always been healthy and beautiful, but my Yorkie was a sick little puppy when I got him. I took both dogs to the vet, and while I was standing in line, another pet owner looked at me with my two puppies and said, "Whenever I see people with new puppies, I tell them having dogs is the best way to prepare for kids. They're expensive just like children, and you have to take care of them just like kids."

Talking with the man made me realize something God had been doing. Throughout my life He had been using various circumstances and experiences to prepare me for the answers to my prayers, but I had to wonder how well I had responded to those opportunities to grow. And how well had I been caring for what I already had—the talents, strengths, abilities, and even the time He had given me? Sometimes it is not just your prayers but how you prepare for what you desire and how you care for what you already have that lead to your victory.

The man was right. Dogs are very expensive and very much

like children, but I have learned that sometimes God will give you something that makes you uncomfortable or stretches you to train you for what is coming. We often give the enemy more credit than he should ever have. That "attack" may be God seeing if you are ready for the responsibility of what you are seeking in prayer.

Pray and keep on praying.

You won't be able to withstand the attacks of the enemy until you are willing to pull out your weapon of prayer and use it. Some people find it difficult to win the ugly fights because instead of speaking up through prayer, they choose to play the victim and remain in silence. We cannot expect a situation to change if we don't give it to God in prayer and keep praying until the answer comes. We often stop praying closer to our breakthrough than we know. Often your fight is not nearly finished when you think it is, and you stop praying too soon and think God chose not to answer.

Jesus commended the persistent widow in Luke 18 who kept taking her plea before the unjust judge until he answered her. We should pray and not give up just because we don't see an answer right away. Jesus said in Matthew 7:7, "Ask and it will be given to you; seek and you will find; knock and the door will be opened to you." I like the way the verse reads in the Amplified Bible: "Ask and keep on asking and it will be given to you; seek and keep on seeking and you will find; knock and keep on knocking and the door will be opened to you."

Don't give up in prayer. Be persistent. Ask and keep on asking.

Lift your voice.

Sometimes the best way to destroy the enemy is to release a shout of praise.

In Joshua 6 God told Joshua He was delivering the city of

Jericho into the hands of the Israelites. Jericho was fortified by high walls, and they knew the Israelites were coming for them, so the city was on high alert. How could the people of Israel possibly win this fight?

God gave them an unusual strategy. For six days He had all the armed men march once around the walls. They brought the ark of the covenant, and seven priests blew trumpets, but Joshua had told the troops, "Do not give a war cry, do not raise your voices, do not say a word until the day I tell you to shout. Then shout!" (v. 10). Then on the seventh day, God had the army march around the walls seven times. "The seventh time around, when the priests sounded the trumpet blast, Joshua commanded the army, 'Shout! For the LORD has given you the city!'...When the men gave a loud shout, the wall collapsed; so everyone charged straight in, and they took the city" (vv. 16, 20).

I bet that shout was something to hear. You have to understand that conquering Jericho was just the first step in taking possession of the land God had promised them. God had already brought the Israelites out of slavery in Egypt, but the unbelief of the previous generation had caused them to wander in the wilderness for forty years, and now it was time for them to go in and possess the promise. That shout was a shout of faith that God would do the impossible. It was a shout of confidence that He would keep His word to them. It was a shout that proclaimed the God of Israel was all-powerful and He was giving them the victory.

Some people like to think God worked one way in the Old Testament and He is doing things differently now. It's true that we are under a new covenant of grace and not the old covenant of law. But make no mistake: there is still power in a shout. There is power in a shout that says, "I believe God will do exactly what He said He would do." There is power in a shout that tells the enemy he is already defeated. There is power in a shout that proclaims the God we serve is mighty and omnipotent and worthy of all praise.

A shout of praise can silence the enemy. Psalm 8:2 says, "Through the praise of children and infants you have established a stronghold against your enemies, to silence the foe and the avenger." The word translated "silence" in that verse is *shabath,* and it can mean "to cause to cease, put an end to; to exterminate, destroy; to cause to desist from; to remove; to cause to fail."[1] When we praise, we exterminate the enemy, destroy the enemy, remove the enemy, and cause the enemy to fail.

I read a story once about a little boy who had been kidnapped outside his home in Atlanta. The kidnapper told the boy he didn't want to hear a word from him, so the boy started singing the gospel song "Every Praise," and he wouldn't stop. The man started cursing and told the boy to stop, but he wouldn't. He kept singing, and after about three hours the kidnapper let him go.[2]

Your enemy is expecting you to cower down and be quiet when you are in the midst of a fight. But try releasing a shout. See how it shakes the atmosphere and knocks the enemy off his feet. Sometimes we have to open our mouths and raise our voices to shut the mouth of the enemy.

Lions are known for their roar. Male lions use it to scare away animals that intrude on their territory or to warn the pride of possible danger.[3] Without their roar, a lion would still be a lion. It would still have powerful muscles and sharp teeth. But it wouldn't seem nearly as ferocious. Raising your voice in prayer is like a roar against the enemy. It lets him know he has encroached on the territory God has given you and God is going to give you the victory. Now, don't get me wrong; silent prayers are wonderful. But Jesus told His disciples to speak to the mountain, not to pray over it silently (Mark 11:23). Sometimes God moves when we release a sound of victory in the earth.

Whether through your shouts of praise or your silent prayers, there is power in your mouth. I find that many times we are defeated because we are too afraid to give a shout in the midst of the fight and truly tap into our victory. Some of the greatest promises came after a sound was made in the earth. I pray loud and proud often so the enemy knows I am never too afraid to communicate with God.

The devil will never force me to be quiet, and I recommend you don't allow him to do that to you either. When you let the devil shut your mouth, you let him close your door—your door of opportunity, your door of favor, your door of promise, but most importantly your door of peace and prosperity—and we can't have that.

When the enemy comes after you and you don't respond with prayer and praise, you set yourself up to lose the fight. Praise and prayer frighten the enemy. Going to God in prayer unleashes His power in your life. Don't let the enemy make you feel as if you aren't powerful enough, strong enough, big enough to fight. God has given you power—in your joy, your peace, your praise, and your prayers—to defeat the enemy. Fight back with prayer, and refuse to let your situation stop you from growing into the person God has called you to be. That's what being a warrior is truly about—overcoming, being able to fight whatever is in your way so you can become the best version of yourself. So prayer is our first weapon of warfare; let's discuss the second weapon.

THE WEAPON OF FASTING

Esther called a fast, asking the people not to eat or drink for three days. Fasting is a way we strengthen our spirits as we surrender our flesh. It is a physical sacrifice that allows us to reap a spiritual reward. Because we put our flesh in submission when we fast, as a result God often releases breakthrough, healing, deliverance, favor, or whatever we have been seeking in prayer.

The Bible tells us some struggles can only be resolved when we fast and pray. In Mark 9 a man brought his son to Jesus' disciples, asking them to cast a demon out of the boy. The spirit kept the boy from speaking and caused him to convulse and throw himself into the fire. The disciples prayed for the boy, but they couldn't cast out the demon, so the boy's father went to Jesus.

After having a little conversation with the man about faith and unbelief, Jesus rebuked the spirit and told it to leave, and the demon obeyed. The disciples were amazed, and when they asked Jesus why He was able to cast the demon out and they weren't, He said, "This kind can come forth by nothing, but by prayer and fasting" (Mark 9:29, KJV).

Some issues are stubborn and more resistant to change, and you have to do something out of the ordinary to see breakthrough. Jesus said sometimes it takes prayer *and* fasting. Fasting helps deepen our faith and strengthen the anointing on our lives, and it is the anointing that breaks yokes. Some things only respond to the higher level of authority and power that comes when you lay something aside and strengthen your prayers with fasting. So if you have been dealing with discouragement, anger, rage, a compulsive habit, or something else you haven't been able to break free of, perhaps it is time to lay something aside.

Most people think of a fast as abstaining from all food and drinking only water, but there are many ways to fast. Some people abstain from meat to symbolize a sacrifice of the flesh and sinful mindsets and activities. Some people fast from sweets to symbolize letting go of the temptations we can so easily fall into. Some people even fast from social media and television, which to me symbolizes a sacrifice of distractions. Distractions swallow us up more often than many of us would like to admit. Distractions take us away from focusing on the things of God, and they are the easiest way for the enemy to gain access to our lives. If the enemy can distract you, he can disconnect you, and before long you will find you are more consistent in checking how many likes you have than in spending time with God. We must learn to recognize the tactics of the enemy!

Just as there is no rule about what to fast, there is no set time frame for fasting. Some people fast for a day, others for three days. Jesus fasted for forty days when He was in the wilderness, and Daniel fasted for twenty-one days. The most important thing in fasting is not how long you fast or what you abstain from but what you do while you're fasting.

Isaiah 58 speaks of the fast God has chosen, and the interesting thing is that it doesn't specify what you should abstain from or how long. Instead, it focuses on the condition of the heart during the fast. In verse 5 the Lord declares:

> Is this the kind of fast I have chosen, only a day for people to humble themselves? Is it only for bowing one's head like a reed and for lying in sackcloth and ashes? Is that what you call a fast, a day acceptable to the LORD?

Fasting should humble us and cause us to search our hearts and repent of anything in us that is not like God. When we fast, we should spend the time we would have been eating or engaging in entertainment praying and reading the Word. The goal of fasting is to pursue God so we can see the breakthrough we have been seeking. The Bible says:

> Is this not the fast that I have chosen: to loose the bonds of wickedness, to undo the heavy burdens, to let the oppressed go free, and that you break every yoke?
> —ISAIAH 58:6, NKJV

Fasting is a sacrifice, so don't stop pursuing God until you receive what you have been sacrificing for. Use the principles discussed in this book alongside your fasting and prayer, and don't give up until your answer comes. Fasting and prayer are powerful weapons for your arsenal, but they are not the only ones. The last weapon threads them both together.

THE WEAPON OF GOD'S WORD

Esther was a Jewish woman who had a relationship with God. She had been taught to fear the Lord, even though she was living in a foreign land. Her cousin Mordecai likely taught her the Word of God and to bow to only the one true God. Her decision to respond to the crisis facing her people by fasting and praying is just one sign she was familiar with the Word of God.

The Word of God is one of the most important weapons because you cannot expect to know the voice of God if you don't read the Word of God to find out what kinds of things God would say. This is why it is important that you not only read the Word but also that you get an understanding of the Word. God said in Hosea 4:6 that His people perish because of a lack of knowledge. You cannot pray with the power of the Word if you do not understand it. Your effectiveness in prayer is built on your knowledge of the Word of God.

Because the Word is so powerful, the enemy sends all kinds of distractions to keep us from learning how to use it as a weapon. Please don't get the idea that the only translation of the Bible you can read is the King James Version. That is simply not true. There are more than thirty English translations of the Bible. Choose one you can understand. The Bible is not just a story; it is a strategy for mankind to be reconciled with God and live an abundant life. When you see it as a strategy, it becomes a weapon.

One key reason to study the Word is to know who God is. But

studying the Bible didn't just teach me who God is and the way He speaks and operates. It also taught me the devices and cycles of the enemy. It taught me the tricks he uses to move us away from our purpose and to thwart our opportunities to become the best version of ourselves—the healthy and stable version. The enemy knows what you like and what you will fall for, so be watchful of the things that often distract you. Be watchful of cycles and repetition in your life because the enemy is not a creator; he is an imitator, although he will try to trick you into thinking otherwise.

Have you noticed that as soon as you decide it is going to be just you and God, all of a sudden the man of your dreams shows up? He looks good and may even sound good, but in time you find he doesn't respect your standards for yourself. He is just there to distract you from your commitment. Maybe it is something simpler. You decide you are going to take back your health, but your neighbor brings over your favorite cake, and you eat it as if cake won't be available after your diet. A very common device of the enemy is every time you go to read the Word of God, get ready for church, or pursue anything that will strengthen your faith, you get tired or your faith is tested and you give up.

That is exactly what the enemy wants. The enemy wants you to get distracted from being great. The reason the enemy doesn't want you to know the Word of God is because knowing the Word helps us recognize the tactics he uses against us over and over again. The Word of God doesn't just teach us who God is, but it also teaches us about our enemy and the many different devices he uses. Your knowledge of the Word of God, quite frankly, can reveal the secrets that will empower you to dismantle the works of the enemy.

Pray the Word

Hebrews 4:12 says that "the word of God is alive and active. Sharper than any double-edged sword, it penetrates even to dividing soul and spirit, joints and marrow; it judges the thoughts and attitudes of the heart." The apostle Paul in Ephesians 6 also described the Word of God as a sword (v. 17), and of all the armor of God listed in that chapter, the Word of God is the only offensive weapon. The breastplate of righteousness, the helmet of salvation, and the rest of the armor defend us against the enemy. But the Word of God is what we use to fight back.

When we pray God's Word, we are reminding God of His promises, and we are letting the enemy know we aren't falling for his tricks. In Luke 4 the Holy Spirit led Jesus into the wilderness, where He fasted for forty days and forty nights. At the end of the forty days, the enemy came and began to tempt Him, telling Him to turn a stone into bread and to throw Himself off a cliff because the angels would save Him. At one point the devil showed Jesus all the kingdoms of the world and told Him they would be His if Jesus would just worship him.

To each temptation Jesus responded with the Word of God, and in the end Satan had to leave Jesus alone. But something else happened. Jesus entered the wilderness "full of the Holy Spirit" (v. 1), but He left "in the power of the Spirit" (v. 14). God's Word not only silenced the enemy, it caused Jesus to walk in a new level of God's power. The same thing happens when we know the Word and use it in prayer. We silence the enemy and grow in the power of the Holy Spirit.

Allow yourself to become one with the Word of God. Knowing the Word will help you in your relationships, your discernment, and your ability to know and hear the voice of God. But most importantly it will help you identify your purpose. Your purpose will not be found in running from your call to the Word. Your power and purpose come from praying, fasting, reading God's Word, and then doing it all over again.

You pray so you can give God authority and open up communication with Him that is authentic and real. You fast so you can sacrifice and be delivered from what is holding your life and mind hostage. You read the Word of God to keep your spirit anchored in the truth. Reading the Word sharpens your mind, heart, and spirit so you can recognize the tactics the enemy uses so often to tear you down, and you defeat him instead.

You don't have to stay broken, and you don't have to be sad. You can do as Esther did and pray, fast, and use God's Word to reclaim your power and rise up as the ferocious warrior you were designed to be. That's right. When you realize ferocious power is within your grasp, you will be able to leap into your destiny just as you were meant to.

Ferocious warriors keep their weapons sharp so they will be ready to attack. Would Esther have taken that walk to the king's quarters to plead for him to spare the lives of the Jewish people if she hadn't been fasting and praying? I don't think so.

Next I want to talk about the heart of the warrior, but before I do, ask the Lord to strengthen you to develop a lifestyle of praying, fasting, and reading the Word of God so you will always be ready to resist the enemy.

PRAYER FOR A LIFESTYLE OF PRAYER, FASTING, AND STUDYING THE WORD

God, I choose to seek Your face in all circumstances. You have given me power to pursue You and to trust You. Even when I felt I lost my power, You gave me a hunger to be strong. God, I pray You help me to apply and activate Your power in my life, spirit, heart, and mind. God, I pray You show me the will and way You have for my life. Show me how to apply Your Word to the situations that seem too heavy for me to bear. Show me how to share Your grace and love with those around me. Help me to apply the fruit of Your Spirit in my life so I can become the person You would have me to be. Lord, I surrender who I am, my will, and my way to You. I give You my whole life, withholding nothing. I surrender my ideas to Your vision and plan for my life. I surrender anything You see in me that is not like You.

I want to be made new again. I want to change my life, and I want to focus on You in a new way. Lord Jesus, help me not to build my own distractions and blame them on other people. I surrender my heart and soul to You. I give myself away. Lord, I sacrifice my sinful ways and thoughts so You can grow me into a ferocious warrior. God, I am grateful that You are able to change my life for the better.

Lord, may my intentions be pure before You. Realign and refocus me so I pursue Your plan for my life. Cause me to reveal Your glory. I need You, God, above all things. Lord, please don't let me lose sight of the role You play in my life. Help me to become better than I used to be. Lord, don't let me hold grudges. Help me to take responsibility for the things I need to take responsibility for. Help me to grow stronger and wiser than ever before. It is so by faith, and by faith so it is. Amen.

Speak Life

For the word of God is quick, and powerful, and sharper than any twoedged sword, piercing even to the dividing asunder of soul and spirit, and of the joints and marrow, and is a discerner of the thoughts and intents of the heart.
—HEBREWS 4:12, KJV

I love the Word of God. I will hide it in my heart and use it to dismantle the works of the enemy. It is quick and powerful, sharper than any two-edged sword, dividing even soul and spirit, joints and marrow. It is a discerner of the thoughts and intentions of my heart.

CHAPTER 8

The P Principles of Prayer

WRITING THIS CHAPTER has been a fight in itself. I have already written it twice, and each time, it makes me feel even more vulnerable.

I have been fighting with prayer since I was little. The first time I remember using prayer as a weapon was when I was a teenager and my older brother Jamar had three heart attacks back to back at the age of twenty-five. When I arrived at the hospital, he was in the throes of the third heart attack, and the doctors could not figure out why. I went to the hospital's chapel and pleaded with God to save my brother from whatever was trying to kill him, and when I walked back to his room, he was sitting up and doing fine.

Seeing the change in my brother showed me what prayer can do. The doctors did not know what was happening, but I chose to believe God knew what was going on, because that is what faith is. So I found a quiet place and prayed that He would heal my brother. I saw God turn that situation completely around, and since that day, I have been fighting the enemy with prayer.

Through the years, my prayer life has been tied to principles that have helped me become more ferocious in prayer. I call them the P principles. Remembering these principles will help you guard your motives, understand your authority in Christ, and anchor your life—not just your prayer life but your whole life—in God so you can be consistent in prayer and persevere no matter what your life may be showing you. Life is going to show us pain and sorrow sometimes, and God is the only One we can truly depend on in those scary and difficult seasons. Instead of running away from God when times get hard, ferocious warriors run to Him through prayer.

We must learn to include God in every aspect of our lives—both when we are being processed and when life seems perfect. If we disregard the P principles, we may find ourselves going through the same tests over and over again and making little progress. So let me explain the three principles that will help you become ferocious in prayer.

CONSIDER YOUR PURSUIT

What we receive in prayer is determined by our pursuit. Some of us pursue material things while others pursue a powerful relationship with Christ. It is important that your prayers aren't laced with a lot of "gimme" but are instead anchored in a true desire to be closer and more connected to God. If you pursue God, not things, in prayer, your whole life will change.

Many of us go to God with a list of wants, needs, and problems, but He loves it when we come to Him just because we want to spend time with Him. Wouldn't you? If you were in a relationship with someone, would you want your significant other to talk to you only when he or she needed something? Of course not. Intimacy is built in all the little moments when you are just spending time together. The same is true in your relationship with God. He loves it when you go into His presence and say,

"God, I don't want anything; I just want to say thank You. I just want to get to know You. I just want to get closer to You."

Every relationship begins with a pursuit. It is how we let a person know how much we like him or her. I had a friend who was very close to me, and whenever things would go bad, the person would ask me for help. But when things were going well, that individual never pursued me; the person's interest was always in what I could give or do. I don't mind helping people, but isn't it nice to be in a relationship with someone who isn't always in pursuit of what you can do? Isn't it nice to have friends who call just to see how you're doing and not to ask for anything?

God feels the same way. He wants to get to know us, and He wants us to approach prayer with the intent to get to know Him. He wants us to put Him at the forefront of our lives. Matthew 6:33 reminds us to seek first the kingdom of God and His righteousness, and everything else will be added to us. Our desires determine our pursuit. If we desire to experience more of God, we will seek His face. If all we want are His benefits, we will only seek His hand.

Proverbs 3:5–6 says, "Trust in the LORD with all thine heart; and lean not unto thine own understanding. In all thy ways acknowledge him, and he shall direct thy paths" (KJV). When you can focus your attention on really acknowledging God in your situation, things start to align properly in your life. You will see God's will and purposes begin to come to pass. But you won't be able to accomplish much in God if you don't look to Him.

Life is not about seeing what God can give you but about taking time to acknowledge Him for who He is. Seeking and trusting God bring a reward, but our priority must be to focus on God and build a relationship with Him.

CONSIDER YOUR POSITION

Nothing scares the enemy more than believers who know their position in Christ. As believers in Jesus we are seated with Christ in the heavenly places far above all principality and power (Eph. 1:20–21; 2:6). And because of our position in Christ we have authority over the enemy. Jesus said in Luke 10:19, "I have given you authority to trample on snakes and scorpions and to overcome all the power of the enemy; nothing will harm you."

Many times we fail to become the best version of ourselves because instead of exercising our authority, we let the enemy make us feel discouraged and defeated. But Jesus conquered the enemy on the cross. Colossians 2:15 says that He "disarmed the powers and authorities...[and] made a public spectacle of them, triumphing over them by the cross." And Ephesians 1:22 tells us that God has placed all things under Christ's feet. Yes, the enemy comes against us while we are still in this earth. But we are seated with the One who has defeated the enemy, and we enforce the victory Jesus won for us through prayer.

At its most basic level, prayer is agreeing with God and disagreeing with the enemy. Whether we are in our prayer closet, worshipping in church, or studying and confessing God's Word, we overcome the enemy by agreeing with what God says and decreeing that truth over our situation. (See appendix B.) The enemy knows you have power over him; that is why he doesn't want you to understand the authority you have in Christ. He doesn't mind if you have heard that "He who is in you is greater than he who is in the world" (1 John 4:4, MEV) or that you are more than a conqueror through Him who loves you (Rom. 8:37). He just doesn't want you to actually believe it or, worse, remind him of that when he comes at you with his lies.

To live in the reality of what Jesus has done for you on the cross, your life must be anchored in God. An anchor holds a boat steady against the wind and waves that might cause it to drift away. To be anchored in God means we tie our hope, our beliefs, and our understanding of what is true to God's Word and His promises. It means we let His opinion of us hold us steady when the enemy and those around us call us everything but a child of God. It means we trust God's character even when we do not know why He is letting us endure so much pain.

If you are anchored in Christ, your life will show it. You will not be tossed and turned by every wave that comes your way. We often think of Peter walking on the water as a great example of his faith. But if you think about it, the only reason Jesus called Peter out of the boat was because Peter did not believe it was really Jesus walking on the water. Peter said, "Lord, *if it's you*...tell me to come to you on the water" (Matt. 14:28, emphasis added). That was when Jesus told him to come.

Yes, Peter's story is an object lesson on faith. He walked on water, and even when he began to sink, the Lord sustained him, and He does the same thing for us. Our God was and still is amazing. But truth be told, Peter ended up out on the water in the middle of a storm because he lacked faith. Jesus told the disciples, "Take courage! It is I. Don't be afraid" (Matt. 14:27), but Peter didn't believe Him. When you are anchored in God, you believe what He says—above what the situation looks like or what people tell you. You believe Him above the doctor's reports. You keep holding on to His promises even when you keep failing the tests to get into graduate school. You believe He is good even when the odds do not look so good. You trust Him when you do not see how He is going to work the situation out. I believe I will give birth to the children God showed me years ago in a dream because my hope and expectation are tied to God and to no one and nothing else.

As a warrior you must know your spiritual position in Christ, but you must also consider how you are positioned in the natural. Are you surrounding yourself with people who are going to benefit you and cause you to grow in new ways? Are you exposing yourself to the right people and the right knowledge to move to your next level and become the best version of yourself? Are you learning how to assume the responsibilities of the positions God has allowed you to walk in? You can be given a position, but if you do not know how to handle it, you will lose it.

Are you standing in God? Or are you letting the enemy distract you from walking in the authority you have in Christ? Are you positioning your weapons so they will be effective against the enemy? If you use the dull side of a sword, it will do only so much damage. If you pray but doubt the whole time that God will answer, you cannot expect to win against the enemy. Position is not just about being on your knees in prayer; it is also about the position of your heart, your attitude, your hope, and your expectations.

Our authority and power are all wrapped up in our ability to trust God and know that He is on our team. Just because someone is on your team does not mean you won't face injury. Think about your favorite basketball team. All the players have a position to play, and the fact that each player does his part does not mean someone won't get hurt. But by working together, they have a greater chance of walking away with the win. I am not saying you are going to win every fight, but as long as you stay surrendered to God, you will win in the end. Don't stay in the position of victim. Embrace your position in Christ and claim the victory.

CONSIDER YOUR P-O-W-E-R

The last principle is power. When we pray, we cannot pray in fear. We have to pray knowing a power rests inside of us that makes us a real threat to the enemy. The apostle Paul wrote in Ephesians

3:20 that God "is able to do immeasurably more than all we ask or imagine, according to his power that is at work within us." The power at work in us causes demons to tremble, which is why the enemy wants to keep us from understanding who we are.

Your power is not rooted in what man says about you. It is rooted in what you say about you. It is rooted in what God says about you and whether you choose to believe it. Your power is rooted in what you tell yourself about your story and your storm, because what you confess is a product of what you believe. Ferocious warriors do not call themselves victims when God says they have the victory. Ferocious warriors do not say they don't have what it takes when God says He is able "to do immeasurably more than all we ask or imagine." Ferocious warriors do not say they cannot overcome that obstacle when God says they are more than conquerors (Rom. 8:37).

Your strength is laced with the things you thought made you the weakest. Second Corinthians 12:9 says God's strength is made perfect, or complete, in your weakness. Your power in prayer is built on the backs of things that were meant to break you. It is built on the backs of things that were meant to take you down. You activate the ferocious power God has placed inside you when you begin to believe what God says about you.

Ferocious warriors are "strong in the Lord, and in the power of his might" (Eph. 6:10, KJV). They stand in His power and don't let anything or anyone keep them from claiming what they know is theirs. I love acronyms, and I have one I like to use that not only breaks down this final P principle but also serves as a guide for praying ferociously. Power is all about passion, objective, the Word, examination, and reinforcements. Let's look at each one.

Passion

David was a great king and a mighty warrior, but he is best known for being a man after God's own heart (1 Sam. 13:14; Acts

13:22). Unlike his predecessor Saul, David wasn't after success or position—he was in pursuit of God. Ferocious warriors are driven by their passion for God. They are not in the fight to win the glory for themselves but to give God glory.

In Psalm 27 David said, "One thing have I asked of the LORD, that will I seek after: that I may dwell in the house of the LORD all the days of my life, to gaze upon the beauty of the LORD and to inquire in his temple" (v. 4, ESV). When it was all said and done, David was after one thing: to be in the presence of God. That is what he chose to seek after.

I love it that David was called a man *after* God's own heart. I imagine David chasing after God, in hot pursuit of more of Him. Our passion determines our pursuit. It is what drives us to keep pressing when we want to give up. Passion is what separates the good from the great in just about every arena of life, and the same is true in the life of a ferocious warrior. Jesus said the greatest commandment is to "love the Lord your God with all your heart and with all your soul and with all your mind and with all your strength" (Mark 12:30). Our passionate pursuit of God is what matters most to Him, and He rewards those who diligently seek Him (Heb. 11:6).

If we draw near to God, He will draw near to us (Jas. 4:8). In 2 Chronicles 15 the prophet declared, "The LORD is with you *when you are with him*" (v. 2, emphasis added). A few chapters later, in 2 Chronicles 26, we read about a young man named Uzziah, who was made king when he was only sixteen years old. The Bible says, "He did what was right in the eyes of the LORD.... As long as he sought the LORD, God gave him success" (v. 4–5).

If we want to walk in power and experience victory, we must be passionate for God. We must seek Him "with all [our] passion and prayer and intelligence and energy" (Mark 12:30, MSG). There are many things in life we can be passionate about—our favorite sports teams, a hobby, or even our profession. But none of those things will make us victorious.

If you want to be ferocious and win the ugly fights, don't lose your passion for God. Romans 12:11 says, "Never be lacking in zeal, but keep your spiritual fervor, serving the Lord." Notice the verse says to "*keep* your spiritual fervor." That means we have a part to play in maintaining our passion for God. Life is filled with distractions, and we must discipline ourselves to keep the fire going in our relationship with God. It is like in a marriage. You have to work to maintain passion and intimacy. Be proactive. Seek God through prayer, worship, and His Word. Ask Him to reveal Himself to you in a new ways. Your passion for Him will propel you to victory.

Objective

An objective is "something toward which effort is directed; an aim, goal, or end of action."[1] We cannot walk in power if we don't have the proper objective. First John 5:14–15 says, "This is the confidence we have in approaching God: that if we ask anything according to his will, he hears us. And if we know that he hears us—whatever we ask—we know that we have what we asked of him." To walk in power, we must pray what God wants and not what we want. Sometimes we think we know what is best in a situation. We think we know what someone else needs or what we need, but it is God who sees all and knows what is best. Giving up JoJo was not what I wanted, but I couldn't pray my will; I had to pray that God's will would be done.

Even Jesus couldn't pray His own will. On the Mount of Olives, just before He was betrayed, Jesus prayed, "Father, if you are willing, take this cup from me; yet not my will, but yours be done" (Luke 22:42). *Not my will, but Yours be done.* Praying God's will and not our own is how we walk in power.

You may be wondering how you can know God's will. God's

Word is His will. We know He wants all to come into the knowledge of the truth because it says so in His Word (1 Tim. 2:4). We know He doesn't want any to perish but for all to have everlasting life because He says so in His Word (John 3:16; 2 Pet. 3:9). We know God wants us know Him and the power of His resurrection and the fellowship of His suffering because it says so in His Word (Phil. 3:10). When we pray God's Word, we are praying His will.

If you try to pray out of alignment with God's will, you can end up blocking His plan for yourself or the person you're interceding for. If you pray according to your own plans or goals, you may pray for the wrong thing. Sometimes we can find ourselves praying for God to let us keep toxic things in our lives that He really wants us to release. To have power in prayer, we must take inventory of our objectives and align our will with God's will.

Word

Power isn't something you fight for; it's something you already have as part of your inheritance as a child of God. As I mentioned previously, Luke 10:19 says we have been given "power to tread on serpents and scorpions, and over all the power of the enemy: and nothing shall by any means hurt [us]" (KJV). God has given us power over the enemy, but we won't see that power at work in our lives unless we apply it by declaring the truth of God's Word. Hebrews 4:12 says, "The word of God is alive and active. Sharper than any double-edged sword, it penetrates even to dividing soul and spirit, joints and marrow; it judges the thoughts and attitudes of the heart." God's Word is powerful. The prophet Jeremiah said, "'Is not my word like fire,' declares the LORD, 'and like a hammer that breaks a rock in pieces?'" (Jer. 23:29).

Nothing scares the enemy like a person who applies God's Word because the Word has the power to break through any obstacle the enemy sets up, any lie he tells, and any chain that has us bound. That is why reading the Word of God can be one of the hardest things to do when we are going through a struggle.

Applying the Word of God is more than reading it. We apply it when we walk in obedience to what it says. We apply it when we spend time in worship because in worship we declare who God is, which is revealed in His Word. We apply the Word when we declare God's promises in prayer, expecting God to answer because "he who promised is faithful" (Heb. 10:23). (See appendix B.)

Applying God's Word is how we activate His power in our lives, but we must apply it consistently. If we don't, we will grow weak and lose our edge in the fight. You gain power when you read the Word and learn to recognize the devices of the enemy. When you know what the enemy is using against you, you will be able to fight against his tactics. But you cannot learn the devices of the enemy if you are always running from the things that make you tired and uncomfortable.

Resistance makes you stronger. When you are going through trials, find a Bible translation you can understand, open God's Word, and apply what it says to your situation. That is what I had to do. I had to dig into the Word and speak it over my life. Applying the Word of God does not just increase your power; it also strengthens your faith, and both faith and power are necessary to become a great warrior.

Every action we take in life will either tear us down or cause us to accelerate to the next level. When you apply God's Word, you can reach a place in life you never thought possible.

Examination

If we want to be powerful in prayer, we must examine our hearts. James 4:3 says, "When you ask, you do not receive, because you ask with wrong motives, that you may spend what you get on your pleasures." If you want to be ferocious and pray with power, you must pray with the right motives, or your prayers won't be effective.

We cannot hide anything from God. We can sound like we are praying fire down from heaven, but if our hearts are not right, God isn't impressed. "All a person's ways seem pure to them, but motives are weighed by the LORD" (Prov. 16:2).

If you question whether your motives or someone else's are pure, ask God to reveal what is really going on. He will let you know. David prayed, "Search me, God, and know my heart; test me and know my anxious thoughts. See if there is any offensive way in me, and lead me in the way everlasting" (Ps. 139:23–24). The same prayer works for both people and situations. Sometimes you will have to release people from your life because their intentions do not align with yours or with God's plan.

God wants us to pray with pure intentions, out of a heart of love for Him and others. So we must examine our hearts, and we must examine our needs. Ask God to show you where you are lacking spiritually. When you know what you need spiritually, you will be able to determine whether new people who come into your life are a necessity, an assignment, or a distraction.

When you have a big heart, you can often allow people into your life who do not need to be there. By the time you realize they are not part of your assignment, you have allowed them into your heart, and they have damaged you emotionally, either by breaking off the friendship or making you feel inadequate. This is the other reason you must examine what you need. If you seek God to supply all your needs instead of looking to people to satisfy them, you won't have to worry about whether the people around you want to take from you or build you up. I know who I am in God, and knowing this has helped me examine my needs even more. I used to gravitate toward people who needed me, and now I point people to God. I focus on needing God in my life and showing the love of God to others.

Reinforcements

There will always be times when we need reinforcements in prayer. Jesus said, "Again, truly I tell you that if two of you on earth agree about anything they ask for, it will be done for them by my Father in heaven" (Matt. 18:19). There is power in joining together with others in prayer. The Bible says, "A threefold cord is not quickly broken" (Eccles. 4:12, KJV).

There are times we need to hold others up in prayer, to use our faith to protect them from the fiery darts of the enemy so they can receive a breakthrough. But there are also times we need others to raise their shields of faith over us when we are too weak to raise our own shield. Or in the midst of a lengthy battle we need others to come alongside us and help us hold up our arms, just as Aaron and Hur did for Moses during a battle against the Amalekites. (See Exodus 17:8–13.) We need other ferocious warriors to pray with us for deliverance and strength and to help us fight our battles.

We need support in prayer, but I have learned from experience that we must find the right kind of support, especially those in positions of leadership. Some people just want to be part of your story for the attention it will bring them. I have learned you have to look for someone who is inspired by you but doesn't want to be you, someone who inspires you but doesn't diminish you.

A good friend of mine once told me to be leery of connecting with people who bad-mouth their previous spiritual covering, because you could be next. That is a true statement. You cannot expect people you have never seen support others to suddenly be loyal to you. Good support is rooted in unconditional love, respect, honesty, and consistency.

The Bible tells us when we walk with the wise, we become

wise (Prov. 13:20). The right prayer support will be someone who wants to see you become the person you have been called to be, someone who believes God's promises and is determined to be ferocious against the enemy. And you might be surprised by the person God brings to walk beside you.

In 2 Samuel 15 David had to flee Jerusalem because his son Absalom was conspiring to take over the throne. Absalom "stole the hearts of the people of Israel" (v. 6) and had a formidable contingent standing with him against his father. When David learned Absalom was preparing to attack him, he fled Jerusalem along with everyone who was still committed to the king.

As David watched his faithful supporters marching out of the city, he was surprised to see a Philistine named Ittai walking with them. David told Ittai to go back: "You are a foreigner, an exile from your homeland. You came only yesterday. And today shall I make you wander about with us, when I do not know where I am going? Go back, and take your people with you. May the LORD show you kindness and faithfulness" (vv. 19–20).

But Ittai wouldn't hear of it and told the king, "As surely as the LORD lives, and as my lord the king lives, wherever my lord the king may be, whether it means life or death, there will your servant be" (v. 21). Despite their differences, Ittai was a faithful ally to David. Don't let perceived differences make you brush aside someone who will be a faithful reinforcement when you are in the midst of battle. Ferocious warriors don't all look the same.

There may have been a Judas in your story, as there has been in mine, but God will bring the right people to support you if you ask Him, faithful people who will help you fight your battles. He will help you discern who truly has your back.

REMEMBER THE SOURCE OF YOUR STRENGTH

When you're in an ugly fight, you need to consider your pursuit, your position, and your power, but you must also remember the source of your strength. Ephesians 6:10 tells us to be strong in the Lord and in His mighty power, and we do that by putting on the full armor of God. The enemy will attack your weakest point in God. If you wrestle with anxiety, the enemy will use fear against you. If you wrestle with anger, he will use your frustrations against you. But by putting on the full armor of God—the belt of truth, the breastplate of righteousness, the readiness of the gospel of peace on your feet, the shield of faith, the helmet of salvation, "and the sword of the Spirit, which is the word of God"—you will be able to "take your stand against the devil's schemes." (See Ephesians 6:11–18.)

You can't beat the devil if your flesh is strong but your spirit is weak. Having on the armor of God will enable you to stay alert to the enemy and remain in prayer. No warrior is dressed without being fully clothed in the armor of God. The enemy's mission isn't really to expose your sin; he wants to keep you from praying, worshipping, applying the Word, and putting your confidence in God. The armor of God helps provide protection and strength against his schemes. Choose daily to put on the armor of God so you will be equipped for battle.

You will become stronger in God the more you lift Him up in your weakest moments. In Mark 11:22 Jesus told His disciples to have faith in God. He didn't tell them to have faith in their skillfulness as fishermen or their education or their families. He told them to have faith in God because He is the source of our strength. What you put your confidence in determines your outcome. That's why we must consider our pursuit. You can put your confidence in obtaining an academic degree or making a certain amount of money or finding the right spouse, but when the enemy comes at you with an ugly fight, none of those things will sustain you. None of those things will bring you the victory. Your strength lies in God, not in yourself or others.

I've seen many people lose not because they were afraid of being weak but because they showed their weaknesses to the wrong people, and the people they trusted used those weaknesses against them. And then there were those, like me, who tried to protect people from their weaknesses and inadvertently ended up taking the place God is meant to have in their lives. I had to learn that my strength is not in my ability to save other people. It is in my ability to step aside and let God be God in a person's life.

We are not doing anyone any favors if we try to take control and fix someone's problems when God wants to use the situation to reveal Himself to that person. Step aside and let God be God. We can lose relationships if we keep trying to play roles in people's lives we were never meant to play or, conversely, if we put others in positions in our lives they were never meant to be in. I have been guilty of trying to be something in a person's life I wasn't called to be, and it affected me spiritually. I learned a lot about myself when I began to pay attention to whom I was drawing into my life and why those who left chose to move on.

KEEP FIRST THINGS FIRST

Your pursuit of God should always be your first priority. Don't let anyone sway you from making Him number one. Let your relationship with God be your anchor. Without an anchor you can easily allow people to control you instead of God. So it's important that you anchor yourself in God by reading your Word, applying your Word, and really making sure you are positioning yourself in such a way that the enemy can't knock you down. You must make sure you anchor yourself in the Word of God and walk in the strength of that Word so your life will show that you believe who God says you are.

When you know what God says about you and who He is in your life, you won't be unstable, insecure, or shaky in your decision-making. God is all we really need, and when we realize He is the all-sufficient One, we won't worry about what people think of us.

I need God. I need access to God, and I will always have that access as long as I keep the P principles of prayer in the forefront. These principles help me live ferociously and be ferocious in prayer. I pray they will do the same for you.

Now it's your turn. I've included a prayer as a guide to help you become more ferocious in prayer. Use it to ask God to help you reposition yourself in prayer by always keeping in mind your pursuit, position, and power in Him.

PRAYER FOR REPOSITIONING IN PRAYER

Father God, I thank You for being God. I thank You that we don't have to worry about being validated or accepted by man because we are validated and accepted by You. Thank You for showing us what we should be after, and that is You. God, thank You for loving us unconditionally, never leaving us when we make mistakes or stray from You, and always going after us.

God, I thank You for strengthening me in this season. God, I confess that I have not always been in pursuit of You and my passions have not always been aligned with Your will and Your way. I confess that I have let go of people I know I needed and that I have been judgmental when I should have shown grace. God, forgive me for persecuting people I should have prayed for. Forgive me for oppressing people I should have lifted up.

Renew my passion for people, Lord God. Bring Your power back into my prayer life. God, show me the way

You would have me to go. Take authority over my life and give me strength. Change the way I discern things, God, so I will try things by Your Spirit and not my own emotions. I bind the hand of the enemy that would make me selfish and self-centered, and I ask, God, that You put me in a place of humility.

I love You, God, and I rededicate my life to You that I may walk in a new power, passion, pursuit, and position. Help me not to avoid the process but to see the promise in the process. In the name of Jesus, it is so, and so it is. Amen.

Speak Life

He makes me lie down in green pastures, he leads me beside quiet waters.

—PSALM 23:2

God will supply all my needs, and He will lead me where I should go for His glory.

CHAPTER 9

Lift Yourself Up

C OME ON, CORA. You have to show her that God is still with you even when things don't go right." This is what I said to myself as I looked at my daughter after the second failed infertility treatment and told her she wouldn't be a big sister just yet. If you have ever felt so weighed down that you didn't know how or if you could get back up again, you know how I was feeling. I was having a "Woe is me! How will I ever deal with this?" moment, and I had to lift myself up from the sadness and sorrow I was feeling to encourage my daughter when what we had been praying for did not come to pass.

Because so many people were praying with us, I thought God would answer the way we wanted Him to. I had to realize that God does not answer in my timing or according to my plans but in His timing and according to His plans. I had prayed for God's will to be done in my life, and He was still working out His plan. I just didn't realize how much pain I would be in through the process. I didn't know that sometimes when you ask God to take over in your life, He will put weight on you and test your strength because "the testing of your faith produces endurance" (Jas. 1:3, NASB). No matter the assignment or how heavy it may feel, God does not put more weight on you than you can bear (1 Cor. 10:13). But being in a relationship with God does not mean there will never be times when life feels a little heavy. As a matter of fact, the exact opposite is true.

There will always be challenges in life. Growing up I was not the cook in the family. I didn't really like the kitchen. Now, if you needed some instant oatmeal, I was your girl, but I would leave the harder dishes to someone else. That was my life until I met my husband. His mother was not just a good cook, she was a chef; so I knew I had to up my game. I had to lift myself up. I had to stop thinking I would never need to be able to cook. I had to stop making excuses. I had to lift myself up out of self-pity and start learning how to cook.

When I start new projects, I want to be absolutely perfect at them, but I have learned that you cannot always be perfect in everything at the beginning. Most of our success is built on our ability to lift ourselves up from a place of fear and pursue the thing God is leading us to do. I watched Food Network for a year and failed at many dishes, but today I can say with confidence that I am a good cook. This is how becoming ferocious in prayer was for me. Instead of letting the heaviness of what I was carrying weigh me down, I had to learn to lift myself up by praying and trusting God.

I remember the first time my father called me up to pray in front of the whole church. In my anxiety about praying before so many people, I looked up to my heavenly Father and, in front of a crowd of saints and sinners alike, said without even thinking, "Dear Jesus!" I had to have been about sixteen years old, and everybody reacted as if that was the cutest thing. But to this day that moment plagues me a little bit. If I could go back to that moment knowing what I know now about prayer, I would have never said, "Dear Jesus!"

I could have easily let that moment hinder me for the rest of my life. I could have chosen to never ever get back on stage to do anything. But I had to lift myself up.

We can get so angry about what we are going through in life that we let the moments of embarrassment, hurt, pain, and failure keep us from moving forward. But if you are going to be ferocious, you have to learn to lift yourself up. Wherever you are in your life, you have to make up your mind: "I will lift myself up out of this spot, and I will be better than when I was down."

DO YOU WANT TO BE WHOLE?

One of my favorite stories in the Bible is Jesus' encounter with a lame man at the pool of Bethesda in John 5. A great many sick people lay beside this pool because at a certain time an angel would stir the waters, and whoever stepped into the water first would be made whole. This man had been lame for thirty-eight years, and every time the pool was stirred, he never made it into the water. The Bible says:

> When Jesus saw him lying there, and knew that he already had been in that condition a long time, He said to him, "Do you want to be made well?"
> The sick man answered Him, "Sir, I have no man to put me into the pool when the water is stirred up; but while I am coming, another steps down before me."
> Jesus said to him, "Rise, take up your bed and walk." And immediately the man was made well, took up his bed, and walked.
>
> —JOHN 5:6–9, NKJV

I find it interesting that Jesus didn't help the man get into the water. He told him to get up, take his bed, and walk. He had to lift himself up, and so do we. No matter how long you have been down, no matter how bad it feels or how lonely you have become, it's time to lift yourself up. If you have been letting your situation control you and keep you stuck, it's time to move on from that place so you can become ferocious.

As I said, I love the story about the lame man. There is so much we can learn from it. In the next few pages I want to draw your attention to just a few things this account reveals about the process of lifting yourself up.

Jesus sees you.

The first thing we see is that Jesus was drawn to the lame man. It is so comforting to know that when we are in a lame state, Jesus is drawn to us. When we are in need, Jesus is drawn to us. Jesus connects with what is going on with us despite where we find ourselves.

The lame man was lying in the only thing he knew, and oftentimes that is what we do. We lie in what is familiar when the reality is we need to get up. The lame man lay in his pain and sorrow. He looked for someone to help him, and when no one would, he stayed in the same place—for thirty-eight years.

We never hear that he tried to drag his body to the water. We never hear that he had been trying to get to the water in any way, but he clearly had enough faith to believe that something was going to happen at the pool because he was lying there waiting.

He was not born there. He had to have been taken there, but he had been lying there and waiting for someone to help him for years. Have you ever just been waiting and waiting for help out of a bad situation and all you could do is trust that something would turn around eventually? That's how the lame man probably felt.

After the first year of nothing, the man could have easily started dragging his body back to where he came from, but he had enough faith to wait there for something to happen in his life. The fact that Jesus will come to our rescue is an encouragement. But endurance is necessary in faith, and this lame man waiting thirty-eight years for something to happen for him shows that he was willing to endure. The Bible does not say for sure, but I believe his endurance is also what drew Jesus to him. He may have given up on getting into the water, but he did not give up being by the water. And because he had not given up hope for a miracle, the enemy couldn't block his encounter with Jesus.

God saw the lame man, and He sees you. He is writing your story in such a way that He is going to step in and take over carrying everything that was once keeping you stagnant and broken and that you thought you did not have enough strength to bear. Just because you don't walk with physical companionship does not mean you are alone. God is watching, and He is with you. He takes care of those who have the faith to trust Him.

You have the power to get up.

The next thing I love about this story is that it shows you have the power to get up. Jesus asked the lame man, "Do you want to be made well?" (John 5:6, NKJV). I don't think He was asking to be calloused or insensitive. I believe Jesus asked him this because He saw how close the man was to the water, yet he had not been in the water. Jesus encountered a lot of people who were in need of help, and in most of those encounters He brought up faith. Of all those encounters, it was the revelation of faith I saw in this story that made me realize how powerful it is.

The lame man was used to people stepping over him. He was used to people counting him out. But Jesus asked him a question, and I believe He was not only trying to find out why he hadn't made it into the pool after so many years, but He also wanted to learn the condition of the man's heart and mind. He wanted to see if the man had faith. Knowing He had the power to heal the man with just one word, Jesus wanted to make sure the lame man was open to receiving healing, open to receiving the truth that there was someone who was not going to walk over him but instead was going to help him.

Sometimes we just need to experience the presence of Jesus in the midst of a long battle that we feel we cannot win. Having Jesus step in to check on your heart and your faith is enough to give you the strength to lift yourself up. No one had checked on the lame man, and when Jesus finally did, He asked him a question to see where his heart was, and then He gave him an instruction: "Rise, take up your bed and walk" (John 5:8, NKJV).

With this instruction the man had to make an immediate decision to change his mind. Jesus gave him an instruction that would force him to act on his faith. When Jesus told him to take up his bed and walk, the text tells us that immediately the man simply got up and walked.

The man could have easily said, "That's crazy. How could You ask me not only to walk but also to pick something up when You know I have been in this place for so long?" He could have easily said, "I can't walk. Can't You see that is why I am sitting here by the water?" He could have even said, "Who are You to tell me to walk?" But the same faith that took him to the water and ultimately kept him near the water is the same faith he needed to take up his bed and lift himself up from his place of victimhood to become a victor.

The power to overcome what he had been sitting in all that time came when he decided to trust the presence of God literally right in front of him. He made a decision to change his mind about the situation. Instead of questioning and second-guessing, he simply took up his bed and he walked. That is faith. It is not questioned. It is not second-guessed. Faith simply is.

Faith will cause you to have an encounter with Jesus through prayer, worship, or reading the Word that makes you completely change your mind and become new. You cannot encounter the presence of Jesus in your life and expect it to not lift you up and help you become better than you ever were before. The man did not give any more excuses after Jesus told him to get up. He got up, and life as he knew it was changed in an instant—all because he believed Jesus when He told him to pick up his bed and walk.

I wonder if we as people have enough faith to look at our situation and say, "It may not have gone the way I thought it should go, but I am grateful that it went." I wonder if we will keep trusting God even when we pray and things do not turn out as we had hoped.

When Jesus told the man to get up, he was instantly healed of a condition he had battled for over three decades. Isn't that crazy? He does the same thing today. You can be dealing with something you have suffered from all of your life, or what feels like all of your life, and Jesus will walk into your situation and ask you to do what seems impossible. That's right. You can be suffering intensely, and God will still look at you and ask, "Do you want to be made well?" Because that is what being ferocious is all about—being able to go through the pain and still pull yourself up when it is time to fight. It is a matter of staring at what seems impossible and mustering up enough faith to lift yourself up to face it without fear.

TAKE UP YOUR BED AND WALK

Have you allowed your condition to control you and keep you from lifting yourself up? The lame man lived this way for thirty-eight years, but everything changed when he had an encounter with Jesus. You cannot lift yourself out of depression and sadness or out of anger and bitterness without first having an encounter with Jesus. Nobody else can make you whole. You have to take responsibility to say, "I need Jesus. I have tried everyone else. I have been searching for people to help me in a situation when I should have been looking to God."

You have to stare yourself down and ask, "Have I been looking for ways to be pitied?" The lame man couldn't blame anyone anymore. He had to take responsibility for himself and say, "I am in charge of getting up." That is what we have to do. We have to own our part in ending up where we are, and if our life or situation is not what we desire it to be, we have to choose to do things in a new way.

You have lain in this place of anger and frustration too long. It's time to fight, but sometimes we look for a way to avoid the responsibility we have in the fight. So we point fingers instead of trying, or we blame everyone else for issues that we didn't believe in ourselves enough to do something about. After so many friends came and left, I learned I had to take responsibility for the way I loved, the way I argued, the way I hurt, and the way I communicated. I had to take responsibility for the way I cried and even the way I forgave.

Forgiveness is tough because it requires us to take responsibility for the role we play, and we then have to lift ourselves up out of the pit we find ourselves in. It can be easier to play the victim than to examine ourselves and really grow up. To be ferocious, maturity is required. You cannot be immature and always think of yourself as a victim and be ferocious in your prayer life. Prayer is not just a matter of asking God to give you things; it is also a way we posture ourselves to give to God. We submit our thoughts to God in prayer. We release our will to God in prayer. We give our praise and thanks to God in prayer. And we give up control to God in prayer, trusting Him to release the answer in His way and His timing.

You are not a victim of circumstance. Sometimes things happen to us because the situation is making us better or stronger. You cannot keep holding on to things just because you feel you are qualified to have them. You cannot keep holding on to your version of a story just because the truth is too hard to admit. Until you have the strength to look at yourself and say, "You know what, I am wrong and I should have never done what I did," you cannot lift yourself up. As long as you attempt to justify your wrong, you cannot make it right. "Everything happens for a reason" can be a way we justify the wrongs we commit. Make sure you are not justifying bad decisions so you don't have to handle what would happen if you took responsibility for your choices and lifted yourself up.

After that second fertility treatment failed, I sat in my parents' family room, trying to swallow down tears as I looked into my daughter's face, searching for a way to tell her she would not be a big sister just yet. Eventually I said something along the lines of: "Sometimes when you pray, it is God's perfect timing, and you receive what you asked for right away. But sometimes when you pray, God isn't done perfecting you, so the answer doesn't come when you expect it. This doesn't mean we stop believing God is able to give us exactly what we prayed for. This just means we have to wait a little longer for God to complete our family, and then Mommy will be able to have babies in her belly."

I never thought adoption would come before biological children, but adoption changed my life. I am a better person having had the privilege of raising Amauri and Jason. I am a better mother, woman, and wife for having gone through the struggles I endured. I have cried, and I have been angry, but I have never regretted the lessons I learned throughout my journey. I learn every day how to lift myself up a little more than the day before.

I have learned how to think like a warrior, act like a warrior, and believe like a warrior. I have learned how to be a ferocious prayer warrior. The only reason I ever wanted to be ferocious was because of all the ugly fights I faced in life. I wanted to learn how to be a threat to the enemy. I wanted to learn how to walk in a courtroom with my head held high, trusting God for victory. And God has taught me to do those things. I have learned to see the negative pregnancy tests over and over again and not cry and get discouraged each time. I have learned that God will strengthen me while breaking me. I have learned to love people even while they are assassinating my character. I have learned to discern people's motives and agenda and to keep the wrong people at a distance. God has taught me all of that through pain and trials.

It's important that we never allow ourselves to become so low in life that we cannot lift ourselves up. You were not born to break. You were not born to lay down and die when you are confronted by something you never imagined you would face. You were born to dismantle the agenda of the enemy over your life, and you cannot do that if you don't lift yourself up. You *won't* do that if you don't lift yourself up. The lame man could have stayed there complaining about everyone who stepped over him, but he was made whole when he had faith enough to believe he could lift himself up. Faith gives you the power to lift yourself up out of your situation. You just have to believe.

When Esther was a little girl known as Hadassah, she learned who God was and what He required of His people. After becoming queen, she understood that she would have to lift herself up in the midst of those who were trying to kill her people. She had to lift herself up to save a generation. If it had not been for Esther's willingness to face Haman, who was trying to kill the Jewish people, she would not have gained even more favor in the king's eyes. Sometimes you have to lift yourself up so you can face the people who are saying you aren't worthy of living. And when you do, you are able to take back what the devil stole from you.

Can you lift yourself up? Absolutely. Will you lift yourself up? That is the question. Esther lifted herself up, and in doing so, she changed the trajectory for her nation. I wonder what you could be holding up for your bloodline by choosing to stay broken in a situation that requires your strength. You deserve to get up. You deserve to grow from this place. You deserve to have life and that more abundantly. But you will never obtain it until you lift yourself up.

Stop pointing fingers and lift yourself up. Stop saying it is everybody's fault but yours and lift yourself up. Be ferocious! That means taking responsibility for your lameness and lifting yourself up. It means taking responsibility for the wrong you have done and walking right. We need to treat others the way we would like them to treat us, and sometimes that's hard. It can be difficult to be the bigger person, especially when someone is maligning you, but you cannot have big blessings if you are not willing to be a bigger person. If you are not willing to grow up, you cannot get up.

Lift yourself up. I know it's hard, and I know you have been in that mental condition for a long time, but you have to lift yourself up. A whole nation is waiting on what God has placed inside of you, and you are wasting time beating yourself up over past mistakes or blaming others when you reap the consequences of your own choices. God wants to do something new in you. You can grow from, and out of, this place; you just have to be willing to do so. Nothing I ever went through was easy, but it was necessary, and I am all the better because I decided to lift myself up.

There are times when lifting yourself up includes letting people go. You do not have to be angry at the people who leave. You can wish them well in their going and let the experience teach you how to make better choices in your relationships moving forward. Our mistakes can make us better if we allow them to.

You do not have to just watch everyone else encounter the

presence of God. Jesus is waiting and willing to speak into your life. You need to be willing to look at your situation and even when it seems unbelievable, tell yourself, "I will lift myself up. I know God's got me. I will not be lame anymore. Now is my season. I refuse to be stepped over any longer. I claim my victory, and I am going after my new walk ferociously." That is what Jesus gave to the lame man. He gave him a new walk. Where you are about to go, you can't be lame anymore. God wants you to lift yourself up so you can leap.

God will prepare a way of escape for you. You can get out of the pain you have been sitting in, and you can get up from the pain and agony of always being overlooked. You can stand up and see the salvation of the Lord. That is what the lame man got to do. He got to stand and see that the Lord was good and that salvation was near.

Don't stay where you are. Be ferocious, and use this prayer to ask God to give you the strength to lift yourself up!

PRAYER TO LIFT YOURSELF UP

God, thank You for giving me the strength to pick myself up. Thank You for loving me enough to want me to be well. God, thank You for coming to my rescue, showing me who I am, and not allowing me to rely on others for what I must do myself. Lord, help me to be who You have called me to be. Lord, I thank You for giving me peace in my situation. I pray, God, that You bind and destroy everything in me that keeps me in a victim mentality instead of being victorious. God, I pray You show me my heart toward others. God, when I am wrong, show me where I am wrong and give me the courage to admit it so that I may be able to become better than I was before.

Lord, help me not to be close to my healing yet not strong enough to reach for it. Help me not to hurt people when I am hurt. Help me to apply the Word to my life so I can heal. I sacrifice and surrender my control so You can rest, rule, and abide in my life. God, I praise You for being my waymaker and my Bright and Morning Star. I love You. Thank You for guiding me into things that enrich my spirit instead of contaminating it. I pray, God, that You give me an eye to observe the things going on around me that would hinder me from lifting myself up. Help me to know who is for me and who is not. Help me to be careful about who I give my favor to. I pray that as I grow and develop in the fruit of the Spirit, You would pour into me and pull out of me everything that makes me less like You.

Give me strength to walk in the victory You have given and to keep people in my life who are going to sharpen me and not cut me. Release angels to help war on my behalf, and give me a desire to reach for You in all that I hope to do, not just for me but for everyone connected to me. Keep my passion for You strong. I will be forever careful to give Your name all the glory, praise, and honor it is due. It is so by faith, and by faith so it is. Amen.

Speak Life

When Jesus saw him lying there and learned that he had been in this condition for a long time, he asked him, "Do you want to get well?"

—JOHN 5:6, NIV

I am not lame. I have faith to lift myself up, and I will lift myself up from this place.

CHAPTER 10

Ferocious Victory

"**V**ICTORY BELONGS TO Jesus"—I hear this song over and over again in my head, even when it's not playing at all. That statement means so much to me because it reminds me that no matter how ferocious I am, I am not the one who secures the victory. The victory belongs to Jesus. So if we want to be victorious, we must maintain a close connection to God because He has the power to change things in our favor. At the end of the day, putting our hope and trust in God is how we win.

Now, *victory* can be defined in different ways. Victory is not just when you win the fight but when you survive all the things meant to destroy you. Going through the small battles shows you how to walk in your small victories.

When Jesus claimed the victory for the kingdom, there were stages to that process. Jesus didn't just come down, get to fighting, and claim the victory. Jesus won a multitude of victories before He ever went to the cross. His victory wasn't just in winning arguments with Pharisees. It was in the face of the blind man who could now see. It was in every doubter who believed His words and in everyone who chose to leave his life to follow Him.

When we consider victory, oftentimes we focus on the celebration, but I want you to consider the ugliness Jesus endured to obtain victory for us all. He was blameless. He didn't do anything except challenge the Pharisees' religious attitudes and their hearts toward those in need. He challenged their faith and offered help to those who needed a win in their lives. Yet one day the religious leaders started devising a plan to crucify Him.

You have to understand that the enemy has a plan for your demise. When those friends and loved ones hurt and betray you, when you lose your home or your job, when you don't have any money, when you are on your sickbed, when things aren't going the way you expected them to go, just know it is the enemy devising a plan to kill you. But what the enemy is using to destroy is really going to unlock your purpose.

There will be times in your life when things will not go the way you hoped they would. There will be times when you feel uncovered, but it's only a test. Jesus was betrayed by Judas, but it was only a test. David felt angry with Goliath, but it was only a test. The woman with the issue of blood felt weak and tired, but it was only a test. Your life may bring you many tests, some in the form of fake friends, some in the form of financial setbacks, some in the form of relationship struggles, some in the form of family issues. All of these things are tests to teach you how to truly rely on God through the process He is taking you through to become victorious.

Judas was Jesus' friend, one of His close companions. He was supposed to be watching Jesus' back, but instead he was looking out for himself and accepted a little bit of money to set Jesus up to be captured. We could most certainly be upset with Judas if we wanted to be, but sometimes you have to thank the people who betrayed you, thank the boss who fired you, thank the bank that denied you, thank the doctor who tried to tell you about your promise, thank the haters in your life who try to tear you down, thank the things that make you uncomfortable because the things that were meant to break you really guided you to your ultimate purpose.

We know Jesus claimed the victory, but it wasn't before going through some ups and downs in His life. Ferocious victory normally comes after many ferocious fights, and ferocious fights can make or break you. Ferocious fights can end up tearing you apart if you aren't strong enough to handle them, but that's the thing—you are strong enough to handle them. You have what you need to win. The things you survive will make you stronger in the end.

When I started thinking about writing a second book, I wasn't sure what I would focus on. I always thought after I wrote *Faithing It* I would get pregnant, and that would make my second book easier to write. As I write this book, I understand even more that my timing isn't always God's timing, but I also know this won't be my last book, and Jason won't be my last child. When I was ten years old, God showed me in a dream that I would give birth to a son named Nehemiah, and I believe I will see that dream become a reality. I believe God put the desire to be a mother in my heart.

If you have a vision and a hope for your life, even if it hasn't come to pass after years and years of believing God, you can't give up. You can't stop hoping. You can't just stop trusting God when things get tough. If I had chosen to not write again until I got what I wanted, you wouldn't be reading this book right now. If you let not getting what you want stop you from doing what you need to do in the meantime, you won't experience victory.

I wanted to have given birth to a baby by now, but that hasn't happened. So you may be wondering, How do you write about ferocious victory when you haven't experienced the victory of pregnancy yet? That is a very good question, and the answer is simple. Ferocious victory is not just a matter of receiving your desires from God. You are victorious when you learn to be grateful for what God has already given you. You are victorious when you let your relationship with God be the source of your strength, joy, and ferociousness.

If you let not having what you want keep you from acknowledging that God has given you all you need, then you won't be able to develop a ferocious mindset, much less pray with a ferocious heart. Your victory in prayer comes from knowing that whether or not God answers you in the way you would like, He is more than able to meet your needs. Ferocious victory comes from knowing that though you may go through ups and downs in life, God will never leave you or forsake you. Ferocious victory comes from being willing to face your battles with the confidence that you have the victory in Christ. When you know the victory really belongs to Jesus, then you can walk into any battle that comes your way knowing the fight is won even before you get in the ring. Because you know I love acronyms, as we near the end of this book, I want to break down the word *victory* to look at what it takes to experience ferocious victory.

CHOOSE TO BE A *VICTOR*, NOT A *VICTIM*

Before we can walk in ferocious victory, we must choose to be victors instead of victims. When we play the victim, we allow things that are far in the past, and sometimes things that haven't happened at all, to rule our emotions and dictate how we handle situations. Those who play the victim are so caught up in everything being everyone else's fault that they wouldn't dare take responsibility for the role they play. People who play the victim make choices they know are reckless and then get upset when things don't work out in their favor. They act traumatized and want your sympathy. They are always looking for attention, often by pretending something is wrong with them when they are actually fine.

Victors, on the other hand, don't let what they have walked through destroy them or keep them stuck in their pain. They want justice, but they don't let their search for justice turn into revenge. Victors take responsibility for their choices and walk with their heads held high. They move forward in the things of God even after experiencing pain because instead of focusing on what they went through, they rejoice in the fact that they overcame.

Your victory depends on whether you choose to play the victim or be a victor. Will you trust God in the situation like someone who knows she has the victory? Will you take responsibility for your actions and use wisdom when making choices? Or will you blame others because taking responsibility for yourself and your choices is so hard?

People who decide to be victims don't take responsibility. They thirst for attention and will pretend there is something wrong with them in order to get it. Instead of becoming better versions of themselves, those who play the victim rely on what I call false victory. False victory lies in always being the one who has been hurt. They will fake an injury so they have to get out of the game, but that isn't victory at all. Whether they realize it or not, people who claim false victory are hurting others by refusing to heal from their pain.

If we play the victim card too long, the grief that made us feel like a victim can fester and grow, and in our pain we will hurt people even if we desire to be healed and change. Being a victor requires us to stand up and take responsibility for any pain we may have inflicted on others. That makes it a heavier responsibility because it means we have to own our mistakes. It's not easy to say, "Yes, I did something wrong, and I shouldn't have. Please forgive me." But it is a key to your victory.

HONE YOUR *INSTINCTS*

Claiming victory is all about what you do instinctively when the battle comes. You can have an instinct to reach for God or an instinct to respond in your own strength. You can have an instinct to respond in faith or an instinct to run in fear. You can have an instinct to forgive those you may not feel deserve forgiveness or you can have an instinct to hold on to bitterness. You can have an instinct to pursue peace or respond in a way that makes a chaotic situation worse.

An instinct is "a natural or inherent aptitude, impulse, or capacity."[2] Forgiveness isn't natural, nor is trusting what you cannot see or pursuing peace. But the more we practice something, the more instinctive it becomes.

We must instinctively turn to God for solutions. We must instinctively let Him show us the right strategy to win the fight. I have also learned we must instinctively choose to forgive. If you can forgive that coworker who gets on your nerves, those kids who did not get it right the first time, the bank that denied your loan, the apartment that declined your application, or the school you did not get into, your heart can begin to heal from rejection, abandonment, and insecurity.

But forgiveness is not just for those who have hurt us. We must also forgive ourselves. If we battle low self-esteem, low self-confidence, or a lack of knowledge, wisdom, or self-control, we will never overcome if we don't learn to forgive ourselves and build ourselves up in God by believing what He says about us, speaking life over ourselves, and accepting who He made us to be. To *forgive* means "to cease to have feelings of anger or bitterness toward."[3] Refusing to forgive and "to cease to have feelings of anger or bitterness toward" yourself because of all the ways you think you don't measure up will keep you from walking in victory. When you can walk in forgiveness, you can become victorious.

There is something else we must instinctively do. Whenever a fight arises, instead of just wanting to be right, we must instinctively work to bring peace. Be someone who wants to bring solutions to chaotic situations instead of adding to the confusion. People who thrive in dysfunction are horrible at initiating peaceful solutions. They don't have an instinct to walk in peace.

You may be in a hostile work environment. You may be having a tough time securing a loan or getting your first place. If your instinct is to fight in ways that bring out the worst in you, you will not get the victory.

The choices you make are important to your victory. You have to be able to make choices that bring out the best in yourself and others. Your choices will either bring good or create chaos in an already confusing circumstance. So the question is, What choice will you make? The choices you make in the midst of the battle determine whether victory is won.

CLEAN BEFORE YOU CHASE

When I was a little girl and I wanted to go out to play or see a movie or do anything, before she gave me permission, my mother would always ask, "Is your room clean?" She didn't ask that question because she didn't want me or my siblings to play. She wasn't trying to ruin our lives, even though at the time we felt like she was. She did that because she didn't want to reward us if we didn't know how to care for what we had.

Before you can chase after ferocious victory, you should ask yourself, "Have you cleaned your room?" Have you cleaned up your life and made sure you are prepared to walk in victory? Have you asked God to bless you with something your life doesn't show you are ready for? Have you asked for a husband but don't like cleaning your house without one? Have you asked for money but don't like saving and budgeting? You have to make sure your life says, "Lord, I am ready to walk in victory. Whatever You say to clean up, I will clean up. Whatever You say I need to remove, I am willing to remove."

Cleaning up your life may mean getting rid of toxic relationships, letting go of bad habits, or truly committing to living God's way. You have to separate yourself from things that could contaminate your victory. You will want to make sure your life is free of people who are bitter, angry, or resentful because they can influence you to be the same way. You will want to make sure your life is anchored in God and His Word. You will want to pursue things that are pure and give you joy.

It's time to clean house. There are things God wants to bless you with, but you have let pain from your past clutter your path. You have let anger over what you didn't receive take away the joy of what you have. You have let jealousy keep you from obtaining true victory. You can chase after victory, but until you take time to look at yourself and see what needs to be cleaned in your life, you won't experience the full reward of victory. Don't let your fear of cleaning up keep you from gaining what God desires you to have.

In addition to clean surroundings, you need a clean heart for victory. If your heart isn't clean before God, you will become a contamination to your destiny.

It's important that you know what your heart is chasing after. David had a heart to chase after God. After the prophet Nathan confronted him about his adultery, he realized his heart wasn't clean. So David asked God to create in him a clean heart (Ps. 51:10). David knew it was not only important to have clean surroundings but also to have a clean heart before God. So he made sure his heart was clean.

We must do the same. Clean your house so you will be prepared for victory.

TRUST THROUGH *TESTS AND TRIALS*

The apostle James said it best when he told us to "consider it pure joy" when tests and trials come because "the testing of [our] faith produces perseverance" (Jas. 1:2–3). The only reason victory is needed is because of the tests and trials we face in life. How you respond to those tests and trials determines whether you will build endurance and maturity and secure the victory. Simply put, if you consider your tests and trials to be something God can use to help you obtain victory, you will move forward toward God's purposes and plans for your life.

If you don't consider your tests and trials to be something that can make you better, you will keep leaning on your own understanding, or what you think is right. The Bible says in Proverbs 3:5–6 to "trust in the LORD with all your heart and lean not on your own understanding; in all your ways submit to him, and he will make your paths straight" (NKJV). It is important that when tests or trials come, and even when they're over, that you always acknowledge God, because He knows the path to your victory. I always say, if you can say God said you were supposed to do something and He confirmed it in His Word, then you are safe. But when you walk according to your own sense of what should be done in the situation, you're leaning on self, and that is not safe. Trust the Lord's ways. They are often the opposite of what we want to do, but they will lead us to victory. Leaning on what we think is right can lead to destruction. The more you lean on God, the safer you will be.

When you are faced with tests and trials, you must walk in truth. The Lord hates a lying tongue (Prov. 6:16–17), and that's because He wants us to live in freedom. The truth will set you free, and lies keep you in bondage. We often lie to ourselves about what is happening because acknowledging the truth is harder than living a lie. But the truth is the only path to victory.

We must swear on the Bible when testifying in court because if we don't tell the truth, we will be committing perjury, and when we commit perjury, we place ourselves in chains. This happens literally in legal situations, but the same is true spiritually.

We can sometimes lose ourselves because we don't want to tell ourselves the truth. We cannot heal what we are not willing to acknowledge. We often miss out on spiritual, emotional, mental, and physical freedom because instead of walking in the truth, we would rather lie. We would rather carry the pain of what we know isn't true than allow ourselves to unlock our chains and tell the truth.

Growing up, I was the snitch among my siblings. That was because I knew there was freedom in telling the truth as I saw it. I would never allow anyone to take the truth from me because I would never allow anyone to take my ability to be free away from me. You can lose your victory if you don't tell yourself the truth. You could lose where God would have you go and what God has blessed you with by living a lie. You cannot gain the promise if you keep pushing yourself into the bondage of lies.

Truth is what gives you victory. Truth gives you access to purpose and favor. If you aren't gaining an abundance of favor in your life, ask yourself, Am I living a lie? Am I lying to myself? Am I allowing myself to be something I am not? Allow yourself to walk in the truth and experience its freedom. Mind you, freedom hurts sometimes because telling the truth to others and to yourself can be painful. But healing from the pain of telling the truth is not nearly as hard as dealing with the hurt that comes with lying. I wasn't a snitch because I liked telling on people. I was a snitch because I would rather get in trouble for telling the truth than for lying. Tests and trials reveal what is truly in our hearts. Remember that the truth will set you free. If you are living in bondage, evaluate whether you are living in the truth.

THE WIN IS *OBVIOUS*

When you're in a fight, victory may not seem like a sure thing, but you are destined to win. Romans 8:37 says, "We are more than conquerors through him who loved us." The word translated "more than conquerors" in that verse means to "vanquish beyond... [or] gain a decisive victory."[1] The apostle Paul writes that we are more than conquerors right after he lists the many things that could try in vain to separate us from the love of God. He says:

> Who shall separate us from the love of Christ? Shall trouble or hardship or persecution or famine or nakedness or danger or sword? As it is written: "For your sake we face death all day long; we are considered as sheep to be slaughtered." No, in all these things we are more than conquerors through him who loved us. For I am convinced that neither death nor life, neither angels nor demons, neither the present nor the future, nor any powers, neither height nor depth, nor anything else in all creation, will be able to separate us from the love of God that is in Christ Jesus our Lord.
>
> —ROMANS 8:35–39

We can be confident in our victory because we can be confident in Christ's love for us. Jesus has secured the victory over those who would condemn us—the people He has chosen—and nothing can separate us from His love. It should be obvious God is giving us the victory. It should be obvious He gave you insight or revelation because He is on your side and wants to show you the path to victory. It should be obvious He wants you to make choices that allow His glory to be revealed in you because He is setting you up for victory.

Here is the thing: what God sees as victory isn't always an

obvious win to us. Two people in a fight expect the same outcome: to win. But to God, both parties can walk away with some level of victory. One person may be the obvious winner of the fight, demonstrating the most skill, the best training, and the best strategy. But the other party is also victorious if she learns something about herself and about God and walks away determined to do better the next time.

"Losing" one battle doesn't mean you don't have the victory. Sometimes the lesson you will learn in "losing" is far more powerful and important than the lesson you would learn in being the obvious winner. Many people who are now business moguls became successful only after embracing their failures. The lessons they learned were more valuable than if they had experienced an obvious victory the first time around. Whatever the win looks like in your situation, your victory is secure. If you trust God through the battle, you will walk away better than you were before. Your win is obvious to God, and I hope it becomes obvious to you.

SPEAK *REVIVAL*

When the prophet Ezekiel was placed in the valley of dry bones, God asked him if the dry bones could live. Ezekiel said, "Only You know the answer to that." Then God asked him to prophesy to the dry bones, and he did, and they began to live. (See Ezekiel 37.) Ezekiel walked away with victory when he was able to look at the dead things surrounding him, speak revival over them, and see them come to life.

You have the power to call the dry, dead things in your life to live again. You have the power to declare the Word of God over your life and watch God resurrect dead hopes, dead dreams, dead business ideas, dead relationships, and dead confidence and self-esteem. Proverbs 18:21 says the power of life and death is in your tongue. If you speak life to yourself in the mirror until you begin to believe what God said, you will never be the same. That is why I included affirmations at the end of each chapter and in appendix B. They are a tool you can use to speak life to the dry areas in your life and believe they will be revived in due season.

Get in a habit of finding scriptures in the Word of God that encourage you and revive you. Start listening to music that revives your heart. Start watching clean comedies to revive your joy. When you start learning how to speak the Word back to yourself, you become a great weapon against the enemy and walk away with victory.

Before you start speaking over your life, ask God to show you what needs to be revived. Ask Him to reveal it to you clearly, and then wait on the Lord. Sometimes the answer will be in the sermon at church or something said during a Bible study class. Or it may be in a song that plays suddenly on the radio and brings clarity to your vision and thoughts. Once God reveals the dry areas in your life, begin to speak life and give God the glory for the change that is going to come.

While you're speaking life, use your mouth to kill the things you know need to die, the things that are keeping you stagnant and broken. Use your mouth to kill the things you know aren't of God and release the things you know He wants to see evident in your life—joy, peace, understanding, and compassion.

It's your season for victory. It's your season for power. It's your season for breakthrough, and I can't wait to see what God is going to do in you and for you. Victory is yours when you begin to look at your circumstances and call forth revival. Speak life to your employment situation, speak life to the cells that may be dying because of cancer, speak life to your discipline so you can steward the resources God gives you. Speak revival so the dry, dead things in your life will live.

GIVE GOD YOUR *YES*

If you are willing to give God a wholehearted yes, then you have won half the battle. You have won in your yes. When you surrender to God, you're saying, "I know I am worthy of walking in peace and freedom. I give You full custody of my life." This must be your posture for you to say: "I give You my yes. I am committed to serving You and no one else. You have my full yes. I will not detour from who You have called me to be. No matter what happens to me, my answer will be yes, Lord." When you can posture yourself to say yes even when you wish you could say no, things begin to change in your life.

I am grateful for salvation, but things didn't really start to move in my life until I gave God my total yes. That was when things began to shift for me like never before. I began to hear God more clearly. I stopped trying to justify my sin so I could get what I wanted, and I laid aside the things that used to distract me and take me down. I gave God my yes, and because of my surrender I know God has blessed and will continue to bless my life.

That's what being ferocious is all about—watching God change and shake your life like never before. I know God's got me. Even when I was not sure of that mentally, something in the pit of my stomach knew. I knew I did not want to keep wasting God's time having Him watch scenes in my life that did not please Him. I recommend that you give God a true yes—not a "yes, but can I still do this and can I still do that?" but a full yes.

Oftentimes the reason the devil is able to attack you is you are playing with God and are not fully submitted to His will for your life. When you can give God a full yes, your whole mindset changes, and God will begin to open your eyes to who He is and what needs to change in your life. I used to tell the young people I mentored, "Don't ask God to strengthen your discernment, bless you, or teach you patience if you don't want to go through any hurt or stretching." When you ask God to strengthen something such as discernment in your life, He will send people who are for you and people who are not so you can test your discernment by determining who's who. When you ask God to strengthen your discipline with finances, you may gain a large amount of money and have to learn how to budget that blessing. When you ask God to show you that He is a healer, you may go through some illness. But whatever you go through, God has given you the power to speak life to it. I have been through a lot of hurt and pain, but I was not able to change my life until I changed my behavior and my heart to say yes to God.

YOU CAN WIN

The experiences I have shared in this book—my struggles with infertility, unproductive relationships, betrayal, and so much more—have all changed my behavior. Your behavior determines whether you will walk out of a situation with victory or not. I could go through life with my head held down because I haven't given birth to the biological children God has promised me. But I choose to believe my victory isn't tied to giving birth to biological children but to being grateful for all the blessings God has brought to my life, even if they aren't the ones I prayed for.

There are levels to victory. Some battles bring a big victory, and some battles bring a small victory, but they are all victories. *Faithing It* was about my process to even believe I could get pregnant despite the surgeries and what doctors said. *Ferocious Warrior* is about how I fought and will continue to fight for everything God wants to birth in me, spiritually and physically. When what God has seeded in you is a threat to the enemy, you are bound to go through some ups and downs, pain and sorrow. But I have learned that as long as I keep my eyes on God, I can win in life.

Now, I still believe and will always believe I will be pregnant one day, but that's not where my victory lies. My victory is in having a man who, even after hearing we would have to battle infertility, told me he would never leave my side and that we would fight and win together. It is in waking up every morning knowing he still loves me and our children, and he is fighting with me and praying for me to birth his child. I have been in relationships with men who never knew my value. I was something they could easily throw away, but to my husband, I am his victory and he is mine. I could not be the woman I am today if I did not have him in my life.

My victory is in having a daughter who is at a master level in all her State of Texas Assessments of Academic Readiness (STAAR) tests. When we adopted Amauri at three years old, she couldn't sing her ABCs, count, or pick out shapes or colors. Now she reads on a high school level even though she is in middle school. That is a victory. My victory is in going to the doctor for surgery that could have resulted in the removal of both of my ovaries and my fallopian tubes but instead having only one ovary removed and having a healthy one remain. My victory is in being able to see the birth of my son Jason and loving him as if I gave birth to him myself. My victory is in having formally adopted him after years of wrestling in courtrooms. My victory is in escaping car accidents that should have killed me and being here to shape two beautiful children into the people God would have them to be.

Ferocious victory is about overcoming the odds, defying the statistics, and winning in the face of adversity. There is a method and a strategy to obtain victory, and it's all about relying on your relationship with God—not your religion; in other words, making your foundation a relationship with God. We have talked about Esther, David, and Jesus, but now I want to take time to talk about you. You picked up this book because you were searching for answers on how to dismantle the enemies you have been facing every day. You picked up this book because you were in need of victory, vindication, or maybe just encouragement.

I wrote this book to not only let you know you can be ferocious but also that you are more powerful than you think. Accept that you are a bigger threat to the enemy than you realize. You are a threat to his tactics, and you are worth fighting for. The Lord decided your life was worth fighting for, and if Jesus decided to be ferocious for you, why not be ferocious for Him? Yes, you could take the easy way out and wallow in the comfortable role of victim. Or you could decide that you are stronger than what you are going through and experience ferocious victory.

I want you to know that the best is yet to come for you, even if it doesn't feel like it at the moment. Even if you have been dealt some difficult cards, you can still have victory. You can still win. I still write letters to the biological children God promised me because I know they are coming. I don't just believe they are coming; I know they are coming.

Victory has no expiration date. The enemy would like to keep you from knowing you are victorious because if you walked in the fact that you are victorious, you would not be able to wallow in being a victim. God wants the things you went through to give you a ferocious mentality, not a victim mindset. Some of the great comic book superheroes gained their powers as a result of something that was supposed to kill them. The things that were meant to kill you are shaping you. They are strengthening and empowering you. Don't give up. Yes, it's hard, and yes, it would be easier to just throw in the towel. But He that began a good work in you desires to finish it. He desires to conquer the enemy. He desires to strengthen you and to keep you in perfect peace. So do not let the enemy tear down what God is building in you.

I take comfort in knowing God would never give me a dream,

desire, or drive to do something He has not called me to do. I have to wait on the Lord, and sometimes that can be a fight. Sometimes I have to fight impatience. We are not always fighting the enemy; sometimes we are fighting our flesh. Sometimes we don't have true joy and peace because we get comfortable in dysfunction. You are so much stronger than you probably give yourself credit for. You were supposed to die a long time ago, but you are still here, and God has so much in store for you.

I want you to know it's possible for you to become exactly who you desire to be, but victory doesn't come without a fight. I had to fight to receive my amazing husband. I had to fight insecurities, low self-esteem, and an overall fear of being hurt to be able to receive the wonderful man God had for me. I had to fight to get my daughter to learn. I had to fight her insecurities and fear of failure. I had to fight to keep my son. I had to fight the pain of losing close friends, and I had to fight unforgiveness toward those who hurt me. I have been fighting my whole life, and I didn't let it break me. I let it build a ferocious faith in me, and I let it make me into a ferocious prayer warrior.

NO VICTORY WITHOUT A FIGHT

You are being built moment by moment. When you feel as if all hell is breaking loose and you don't know your end from your beginning, you are being built in that moment. You are a violent threat to the enemy. That is why he is pulling out all the stops to bring you down. But you have authority to tread over the enemy and be victorious over every obstacle he brings into your life.

The Bible tells us in Luke 10:19 that God has given us the authority to tread over scorpions and serpents and overcome all the power of the enemy, and nothing will by any means harm us. It's one thing to know the Word; it's another to walk in it. People who are ferocious tread over the enemy, knowing that nothing will harm them. This idea is repeated more than once in Scripture. Isaiah 54:17 says, "No weapon formed against you shall prosper" (NKJV). And God declared in Isaiah 41:10, "Do not fear, for I am with you; do not be dismayed, for I am your God. I will strengthen you and help you; I will uphold you with my righteous right hand." No matter what the problem looks like, we are never told to be afraid. The Bible tells us again and again to fear not. (See also Isaiah 41:13–14; 43:1–5; and John 14:27.)

Fear isn't a factor when you are ferocious. The major battle to become a ferocious warrior is not to fear. That is why you must have ferocious faith, use the weapons of a warrior, including the P and D principles, and think like a warrior. Your life is going to be a series of battles. Some you will win, and some you will lose, but all of them are sent to help you mature and become the person God made you to be. I call that the best version of yourself; it's the you God knows you can be.

Don't let people deter you from your destiny because of their fear of reaching their own. It is never your responsibility to make someone else comfortable with what God is doing in you. Ferocious victory is part of your destiny. Just believe it, and you will receive it. Just consider the story of the woman in Luke 13 who had been crippled for eighteen years. "She was bent over and could not straighten up at all" (v. 11), but she was still going to synagogue. Isn't that something? Some people can be hurt for a minute and leave the church altogether. This woman had been bent over for eighteen years, and she was still going to synagogue and trying to praise and worship God. She didn't let her condition keep her from reaching for more of God.

One day when she was in the synagogue, Jesus saw her, called her over, and told her, "Woman, thou art loosed from thine infirmity" (v. 12, KJV). This is the story that birthed my father's "Woman, Thou Art Loosed" message, which became his first best-selling book and started one of his largest conferences worldwide. The woman in the Bible received victory because she was ferocious enough to go into an environment with an ear to hear the Word and a heart to receive the Word despite her physical condition.

I guess you are wondering why this is important for you to know. It's because often in life you will be crippled, and you cannot let that stop you from reaching for God and allowing Him to touch you. Your brokenness does not have to block you from God's power. In fact, it can do the exact opposite if you allow it to. You are designed to grow beyond the confines of what has crippled you. You are designed to receive victory. I don't care if it has been eighteen years, twelve years, thirty-eight years, or three days—you are designed to rise up from situations that were meant to kill you. Don't give up or throw in the towel. If you are willing to lift yourself up from your broken state and let God be God in your life, you will win.

I can't wait to see how you live your life ferociously. You can have ferocious prayers, ferocious faith, and most importantly a ferocious lifestyle, and in having a ferocious lifestyle, you will truly dismantle the enemy, no matter how ugly the fight. Everything I have written in this book, all the prayers and teaching, is designed to help you develop a ferocious lifestyle. You don't have to be afraid anymore because you are a conqueror. Yes, it's easier said than done, but that is often just an excuse not to conquer. You cannot spend your life always trying. At some point you have to say, "You know what, I need to stop always trying, and I need to finally do it. I need to stop saying, 'I will,' and really walk toward what I desire."

I didn't become ferocious by trying; I became ferocious by doing. Every time I felt myself trying to become something I didn't want to be, I would challenge that mindset with prayer and the Word of God. I have spent the last several chapters giving you every method that helped me become the ferocious prayer warrior I am today. By now you ought to be ready to not run from the enemy but to walk in a new you, take on the obstacles of life, and ferociously destroy the works of the enemy. Let the following prayer strengthen and encourage you. Use it to ask God to help you develop a ferocious lifestyle.

PRAYER FOR A FEROCIOUS LIFESTYLE

Spirt of the living God, I honor and adore You. I give You praise for who You are in my life. You are amazing, marvelous, wonderful, pure, a blessing, and a chain breaker. You are honest, loving, gracious, and powerful, and for this I give You all the praise. Thank You for being loyal, enduring, and my joy and strength when I am weak. Thank You for having Your hand on my life.

I confess that my choices have not always honored You, but I choose faith over fear from this day on. I choose to draw closer to You and to pursue what pleases You and not merely what pleases my lustful desires. I thank You for forgiving me and loving me unconditionally. I thank You for giving me peace in the midst of my storms and for bestowing blessings and privileges I don't deserve. Thank You for always keeping Your arms open to me and for never leaving or forsaking me.

God, I ask that You create in me a clean heart and renew a right spirit in me. Bind every wicked thing in me, seen and unseen, and destroy it from the root from all generations that came before me all the way back to Adam. Destroy every strongman and worker of iniquity that may be housed in my soul and keeping me from moving forward in You. God, help me to reverence the role You play in the very breath I breathe every single day of my life.

God, help me to walk victoriously and not as a victim of circumstance. Help me to know what to initiate and what not to initiate. Help me to know when to take the initiative to present a solution and when to walk away. Lord, help me to be cognizant of my choices and to make choices that will help me become a better person. Lord, help me walk in truth and power that I may be free from the bondage of things I know aren't true about me. God, help me to see what is obvious in Your Word concerning me and my situation. Lord, give me the ability to see the devices of the enemy from afar and to respond with divine wisdom and power.

God, help me not to hurt others in my hurt, and help me not to become comfortable in dysfunction and tear other people down. Transform me. Transform my heart and mind until I see things differently and can see my surroundings more clearly. God, restore my faith in You. Help me to know what to revive in my life and what to let die. I want to walk in liberty and freedom like never before. Remove every spirit of anger that may keep me from trusting You completely.

Lord God, I ask You to open up a new opportunity for me to see the power of Your hand over my life. I ask, O God, that You help me move in a direction that lines up with Your plan for my life. Help me to hear You clearly and to trust what You are saying, Lord God. Cleanse my ear gates and eye gates from all things that may be sent to contaminate me and rob me of my destiny. God, wash me from the inside out so I will have a ferocious lifestyle. Remove every resistant spirit that keeps me from submitting to Your Word.

God, give me clarity of thought and clarity of vision. God, I block every word curse I have spoken or that has been spoken over me that takes away my voice and power. I surrender unforgiveness, bitterness, anger, doubt, laziness, excuses, immaturity, victimization, guilt, lying, and everything else I know isn't like You. Burn it with the fire of the Holy Ghost. Help me become more like You every day—to walk more like You and to trust You more.

I decree and declare my destiny is fruitful. I bind and destroy every spirit of barrenness, and I decree and declare my purpose is fruitful. Thank You for being who You are. I receive all You have for me in this season, and I ask that You give me strength to bear the weight of it all. In the mighty name of Jesus, I decree a new beginning over my bloodline. Things will begin to change. Things will begin to turn around. God will begin to shift things in my life. In the name of Jesus, it is so by faith, and by faith so it is. Amen.

Speak Life

I have given you authority to trample on snakes and scorpions and to overcome all the power of the enemy; nothing will harm you.

—LUKE 10:19

I am ferocious, and because I am ferocious, I choose to tread and trample over all that attacks me, and nothing will harm me. I have ferocious faith; I am a ferocious prayer warrior. I live a ferocious lifestyle.

Conclusion

MANY TIMES WHEN I was a little girl, my father and mother would call all of us kids into the living room, and my father would sit us down and read us a story. I absolutely love hearing my father tell a story because his voice is so authoritative and ferocious.

We know of most warriors, both real and fictional, because of their stories. The tales of their bravery, determination, and exploits captivate us. We are amazed at the odds they overcame to secure the victory or the simple things that led to their defeat. Whether Samson or David, Spartacus or Joan of Arc, their stories leave us enraptured and wanting to know more.

Like legends and icons, the warriors we have learned about in the Bible live on because of their stories, and one of my favorites is the woman with the issue of blood. I've referred to her story a few times in this book because I have always been able to relate to her so much. Her story shows that maintaining faith in the midst of life's obstacles can bring power, prosperity, and peace. When life brought me tests, I thought about the woman with the issue of blood and, knowing God could bring healing, I began to seek Him ferociously. I have learned that life's tests teach us how to survive, suffer, and succeed. I am a warrior because I chose survival in the face of situations that should have killed all my hopes and dreams. And surviving has given me a story.

You too have a story that will change the world, a story that speaks to the times you survived some of the most trying tests and trials in life to obtain what is rightfully yours—your prosperity, your peace, and most importantly your power. That is why I love the woman with the issue of blood. We never learn her name, but we know she left her condition with power, prosperity, and peace.

This book has been about how I erupted from the shadows of pain, barrenness, and the scrutiny of being a celebrity preacher's daughter and became a ferocious warrior who battles by faith, prayer, and power. Although I have a well-known and anointed father, my power does not come from being T. D. Jakes' daughter. My power is in being God's daughter. Embracing the fact that I am God's daughter has taken me to a whole new level in life, and it created my story. When I was willing to go after God with everything in me—all my heart, mind, soul, and strength—I discovered my crown as a daughter of the King.

I was once a broken woman, and I am so glad this book gave me an opportunity to tell you how I discovered power and faith. As you have seen, my life has been filled with many tosses and turns. I never thought Jesus would reveal Himself to me when I was battling infertility. I thought I would be left alone and never receive my promises. But through that battle, I have been given an opportunity to be a blessing to others. The reality is Jesus has used the ugly fights to make me better than I was before.

What I thought was one battle became an all-out war with no end in sight. You know my story. I went to doctor after doctor, but nothing and no one could help me. Suddenly the weight of my issue became so big and strong that I felt like every day I was being crushed by this burden on my shoulder. Before I knew it, I was becoming untouchable and hard to love, and I was accumulating new burdens day by day. Because I was letting my issues consume me, I was losing my sense of who I was. I have since learned that when things happen in your life that detour you from the life you thought you would have or the life you have known, you have to pursue wholeness. You have to reach for Jesus just as the woman with the issue of blood did.

Pain, problems, and processing were part of my story. But I kept pushing and praying, and God showed up for me, and I know He will continue to show up for me as long as I am relentless for Him and willing to go to war against the enemy. Through it all I learned how not to be afraid of the enemy, and I hope that in these last moments we have that you too are walking away knowing your pain and tests of faith are what make you a great warrior. You have a story to tell, so tell the story of how you became a warrior. Let people know what you could have never overcome without God. This may seem like the worst thing you have ever experienced, but you will get through it. God's power hasn't changed. He is just adding to your story.

When I was being hit on every side in my life, faith kept telling me not to give up because sooner or later something would work out for me. I could have wasted time wondering why I wasn't dead yet since my body had been through so much turmoil. But now I realize my body was subject to a process I had no control over. Perhaps you've felt that way before, or maybe you feel that way right now—like you're stuck in a process in life you have no control over and that you aren't sure you will ever get out of. This is what I call the bleeding process in the story of the warrior. We never know what caused the woman with the issue of blood to hemorrhage for twelve years, but we know her bleeding led her to reach for the Savior. Yes, the bleeding process is painful, but through it God is making you into something you never thought you would become.

The woman with the issue of blood didn't just touch Him; she fastened to Jesus. Whatever you are going through, if you are bleeding, then you must connect with Jesus. You must reach out for the truth of who He says you are and tap into the power

He has placed within you. You don't need to die in this bleeding state. This is just a part of your story, not the end. Like every good story, yours has an arc—a beginning, a middle, and an end. This is the part of your story where you develop into the warrior you will become. You will fight and win the battle, you will continue your success, and you will tell the story.

Just keep Jesus in the center of your thoughts and God's Word in your ears. Don't forget your strategy and your weapons. And remember to stay diligent, dedicated, and disciplined to overcome and dismantle the enemy's schemes against you. That's how you become a ferocious warrior.

I sometimes imagine the thoughts going through the head of the woman with the issue of blood as she moved toward Jesus. Maybe the enemy told her, "If you so much as think of touching this man while you are bleeding, it could lead to your death. He is a rabbi, and you can't touch Him while you are bleeding." I am sure she struggled with the decision, wondering if she should take the risk. But in the end she chose to reach for Him.

Your decisions will always affect your destiny, and you decide to what magnitude it is affected. You will face many battles, and the question is, Will you reach out to Jesus in the midst of the battle and become ferocious?

You are stronger than you think. You are a mighty warrior, and you must embrace that your whole story from this moment forward has changed. If you choose to use the methods, strategies, and tools in this book, you won't just be a warrior—you'll be a ferocious warrior.

Until we meet again, fight strong, fight with faith, and never, ever give up. I send you off with this prayer to encourage you and seal the warrior in you.

PRAYER TO SEAL THE WARRIOR IN YOU

God, I thank You for the warrior You have placed inside of me. I thank You for every scar and every loss I have endured. I thank You for every problem that has taught me something. I thank You for seeing me as more than a conqueror and causing Your strength to rise up in me. I thank You for stirring up the gifts in me that make me a great warrior. I thank You for sealing every area in my life that has been left open to the enemy. I thank You for closing those doors and making things new in me again.

I thank You for making me ferocious and building me up to be ferocious. I pray, God, that You would cause hope to be renewed in my life and that my expectations will begin to rise. I thank You for opening new doors for me that will cause me to grow and develop like never before. I thank You, Lord, that today will be a day of love and prosperity for me, and I am grateful that You are leading me to peace. I cast down anything in me and in my bloodline that pulls me away from You, O Lord. Thank You, Lord, for keeping me in perfect peace. I believe You are doing a new thing in me. It is so, and so it is. Amen.

Who You Are in Christ

KNOWING WHO YOU are in Christ will allow you to counteract lies about who and what you are with the truth of God's Word. As a believer in Jesus Christ, the risen Son of God, you are:

A CHILD OF GOD

The Spirit himself testifies with our spirit that we are God's children.

—ROMANS 8:16

See what great love the Father has lavished on us, that we should be called children of God! And that is what we are!

—1 JOHN 3:1

AN OVERCOMER

For everyone born of God overcomes the world. This is the victory that has overcome the world, even our faith.

—1 JOHN 5:4

They overcame him by the blood of the Lamb and by the word of their testimony.

—REVELATION 12:11, MEV

CHOSEN

You did not choose me, but I chose you and appointed you so that you might go and bear fruit—fruit that will last—and so that whatever you ask in my name the Father will give you.

—JOHN 15:16

But you are a chosen people, a royal priesthood, a holy nation, God's special possession, that you may declare the praises of him who called you out of darkness into his wonderful light.

—1 PETER 2:9

COMPLETE

So you also are complete through your union with Christ, who is the head over every ruler and authority.

—COLOSSIANS 2:10, NLT

Let perseverance finish its work so that you may be mature and complete, not lacking anything.

—JAMES 1:4

DELIVERED

I sought the LORD, and he answered me; he delivered me from all my fears.

—PSALM 34:4

He has delivered us from the domain of darkness and transferred us to the kingdom of his beloved Son, in whom we have redemption, the forgiveness of sins.

—COLOSSIANS 1:13–14, ESV

FEARFULLY AND WONDERFULLY MADE

For you created my inmost being; you knit me together in my mother's womb. I praise you because I am fearfully and wonderfully made.

—PSALM 139:13–14

FREE

So if the Son sets you free, you will be free indeed.

—JOHN 8:36

It is for freedom that Christ has set us free. Stand firm, then, and do not let yourselves be burdened again by a yoke of slavery.

—GALATIANS 5:1

GOD'S HANDIWORK

For we are God's handiwork, created in Christ Jesus to do good works, which God prepared in advance for us to do.

—EPHESIANS 2:10

GUARDED

The LORD will go before you, the God of Israel will be your rear guard.

—ISAIAH 52:12

But the Lord is faithful; he will strengthen you and guard you from the evil one.

—2 THESSALONIANS 3:3, NLT

HEALED

I am the LORD, who heals you.

—EXODUS 15:26

But he was pierced for our transgressions, he was crushed for our iniquities; the punishment that brought us peace was on him, and by his wounds we are healed.

—ISAIAH 53:5

KNOWN

But now, this is what the LORD says—he who created you, Jacob, he who formed you, Israel: "Do not fear, for I have redeemed you; I have summoned you by name; you are mine.

—ISAIAH 43:1

Nevertheless, God's solid foundation stands firm, sealed with this inscription: "The Lord knows those who are His."

—2 TIMOTHY 2:19

LOVED

I have loved you with an everlasting love; I have drawn you with unfailing kindness.

—JEREMIAH 31:3

But God demonstrates his own love for us in this: While we were still sinners, Christ died for us.

—ROMANS 5:8

MORE THAN A CONQUEROR

In all these things we are more than conquerors through him who loved us.

—ROMANS 8:37

NO LONGER A SLAVE TO FEAR

The Spirit you received does not make you slaves, so that you live in fear again; rather, the Spirit you received brought about your adoption to sonship. And by him we cry, "Abba, Father."

—ROMANS 8:15

PROTECTED

You are my hiding place; you will protect me from trouble and surround me with songs of deliverance.

—PSALM 32:7

He will cover you with his feathers. He will shelter you with his wings. His faithful promises are your armor and protection.

—PSALM 91:4, NLT

SHELTERED

For in the day of trouble he will keep me safe in his dwelling; he will hide me in the shelter of his sacred tent and set me high upon a rock.

—PSALM 27:5

Whoever dwells in the shelter of the Most High will rest in the shadow of the Almighty. I will say of the LORD, "He is my refuge and my fortress, my God, in whom I trust."

—PSALM 91:1–2

STRENGTHENED

He gives strength to the weary and increases the power of the weak. Even youths grow tired and weary, and young men stumble and fall; but those who hope in the LORD will renew their strength. They will soar on wings like eagles; they will run and not grow weary, they will walk and not be faint.

—ISAIAH 40:29–31

I can do all this through him who gives me strength.

—PHILIPPIANS 4:13

VALUABLE

And the very hairs on your head are all numbered. So don't be afraid; you are more valuable to God than a whole flock of sparrows.

—LUKE 12:7, NLT

VICTORIOUS

Now this I know: The LORD gives victory to his anointed. He answers him from his heavenly sanctuary with the victorious power of his right hand.

—PSALM 20:6

But thanks be to God! He gives us the victory through our Lord Jesus Christ.

—1 CORINTHIANS 15:57

Scriptures and Declarations to Awaken the Warrior in You

EVERY TIME YOU declare God's Word over your life or your situation, you become a weapon against the enemy. Use the following scriptures and declarations to proclaim your ferocious victory over your enemy.[1]

I refuse to live in fear.

> God has not given us a spirit of fear, but of power and of love and of a sound mind.
>
> —2 TIMOTHY 1:7, NKJV

> Fear not, for I have redeemed you; I have called you by your name; you are Mine. When you pass through the waters, I will be with you; and through the rivers, they shall not overflow you. When you walk through the fire, you shall not be burned, nor shall the flame scorch you. For I am the LORD your God, the Holy One of Israel, your Savior.
>
> —ISAIAH 43:1–3, NKJV

> Even though I walk through the darkest valley, I will fear no evil, for you are with me.
>
> —PSALM 23:4

> I sought the LORD, and he answered me; he delivered me from all my fears.
>
> —PSALM 34:4

> When I am afraid, I put my trust in you.
>
> —PSALM 56:3

> There is no fear in love. But perfect love drives out fear, because fear has to do with punishment. The one who fears is not made perfect in love.
>
> —1 JOHN 4:18

I will not be intimidated by the enemy. God did not give me a spirit of fear; He gave me a spirit of power and of love, and a sound, disciplined mind. I do not run from my enemies. I face them with ferocious faith because my God is with me. He has redeemed me and called me by His name. I belong to Him. When I go through the waters, I will not be overwhelmed. When I go through the fire, I will not be burned, because God is my Savior. I will trust God when I am afraid. God's perfect love casts out all fear in my heart. I am fearless and ferocious. I will walk in my destiny, pursue my dreams, and become the person God made me to be.

I choose to live by faith.

> And without faith it is impossible to please God, because anyone who comes to him must believe that he exists and that he rewards those who earnestly seek him.
>
> —HEBREWS 11:6

> Be on your guard; stand firm in the faith; be courageous; be strong.
>
> —1 CORINTHIANS 16:13

> But blessed is the one who trusts in the LORD, whose confidence is in him.
>
> —JEREMIAH 17:7

> But my righteous one will live by faith. And I take no pleasure in the one who shrinks back.
>
> —HEBREWS 10:38

I will move forward as God leads, even if I don't have all the details figured out. Walking by faith is a choice, and I choose to live by faith. My confidence is in God and His love for me. I am strong in the Lord and in the power of His might. I stand firm in faith, strong and courageous, because God takes no pleasure in those who shrink back from Him. Without faith it is impossible to please God. But those who put their confidence in God are blessed. I choose to be blessed because I choose to put my faith in God.

I will not give up in the midst of opposition.

> Consider it pure joy, my brothers and sisters, whenever you face trials of many kinds, because you know that the testing of your faith produces perseverance.
>
> —JAMES 1:2–3

> The LORD himself goes before you and will be with you; he will never leave you nor forsake you. Do not be afraid; do not be discouraged.
>
> —DEUTERONOMY 31:8

> Be strong and courageous. Do not be afraid; do not be
> discouraged, for the LORD your God will be with you
> wherever you go.
>
> —JOSHUA 1:9

I will not be discouraged in the midst of trials because the Lord
is with me. He will never leave me nor forsake me. I will not be
dismayed because I know the testing of my faith produces perseverance. I will be strong and courageous.

I believe God's Word, and it is powerful.

> For the word of God is quick, and powerful, and sharper
> than any twoedged sword, piercing even to the dividing
> asunder of soul and spirit, and of the joints and marrow,
> and is a discerner of the thoughts and intents of the heart.
>
> —HEBREWS 4:12, KJV

> Faith comes by hearing, and hearing by the word of God.
>
> —ROMANS 10:17, NKJV

> Do not merely listen to the word, and so deceive your-
> selves. Do what it says. Anyone who listens to the word
> but does not do what it says is like someone who looks
> at his face in a mirror and, after looking at himself, goes
> away and immediately forgets what he looks like. But who-
> ever looks intently into the perfect law that gives freedom,
> and continues in it—not forgetting what they have heard,
> but doing it—they will be blessed in what they do.
>
> —JAMES 1:22–25

I love the Word of God. I will hide it in my heart and use it to dismantle the works of the enemy. It is quick and powerful, sharper
than any two-edged sword, dividing even soul and spirit, joints
and marrow. It is a discerner of the thoughts and intentions of
my heart. I do not merely listen to the Word; I do what it says.

I believe what God says about me.

> For you created my inmost being; you knit me together in my mother's womb. I praise you because I am fearfully and wonderfully made.
>
> —Psalm 139:13–14

> "For I know the plans I have for you," declares the Lord, "plans to prosper you and not to harm you, plans to give you hope and a future."
>
> —Jeremiah 29:11

> For as he thinketh in his heart, so is he.
>
> —Proverbs 23:7, kjv

> Do not conform to the pattern of this world, but be transformed by the renewing of your mind. Then you will be able to test and approve what God's will is—his good, pleasing and perfect will.
>
> —Romans 12:2

> Finally, brethren, whatsoever things are true, whatsoever things are honest, whatsoever things are just, whatsoever things are pure, whatsoever things are lovely, whatsoever things are of good report; if there be any virtue, and if there be any praise, think on these things.
>
> —Philippians 4:8, kjv

I choose to meditate on the things that are true. I reject all lies and am transformed by the renewing of my mind. I believe what God's Word says about me. God's Word says His thoughts about me are precious (Ps. 139:17), that He rejoices over me (Isa. 62:5; Zeph. 3:17), and that I am fearfully and wonderfully made (Ps. 139:14). I choose to believe God's Word concerning me because as I think in my heart so am I.

I trust God.

> Trust in the LORD with all your heart and lean not on
> your own understanding; in all your ways submit to him,
> and he will make your paths straight.
>
> —PROVERBS 3:5–6

> Trust in the LORD, and do good; dwell in the land and
> befriend faithfulness. Delight yourself in the LORD, and
> he will give you the desires of your heart. Commit your
> way to the LORD; trust in him, and he will act. He will
> bring forth your righteousness as the light, and your jus-
> tice as the noonday. Be still before the LORD and wait
> patiently for him; fret not yourself over the one who pros-
> pers in his way, over the man who carries out evil devices!
>
> —PSALM 37:3–7, ESV

> Trust in him at all times, you people; pour out your
> hearts to him, for God is our refuge.
>
> —PSALM 62:8

I will trust in the Lord at all times. I believe He has good plans
for me. Even when I don't understand why I am going through
what I'm facing, I trust His heart for me. I will confide in Him
because I know He is concerned about every aspect of my life. As
I delight myself in Him, He will give me the desires of my heart.
I submit my way to Him, and He brings forth my righteousness.

I surrender my life to God.

> Surrender your heart to God, turn to him in prayer, and
> give up your sins—even those you do in secret. Then you
> won't be ashamed; you will be confident and fearless.
>
> —JOB 11:13–15, CEV

> I beseech you therefore, brethren, by the mercies of God, that you present your bodies a living sacrifice, holy, acceptable to God, which is your reasonable service.
>
> —ROMANS 12:1, NKJV

> Be still and know (recognize, understand) that I am God. I will be exalted among the nations! I will be exalted in the earth.
>
> —PSALM 46:10, AMP

> Then he said to them all: "Whoever wants to be my disciple must deny themselves and take up their cross daily and follow me. For whoever wants to save their life will lose it, but whoever loses their life for me will save it."
>
> —LUKE 9:23–24

I present myself to God as a living sacrifice, which is my reasonable service. I give God my plans and yield to His will for me. I recognize that He is God and I am not. I renounce all forms of rebellion and humbly take up my cross and follow Him. I submit to God's authority in my life. Because I surrender my heart to Him, I will not be ashamed; I will be confident and fearless.

God is my strength.

> For You have girded me with strength for battle; You have subdued under me those who rose up against me.
>
> —PSALM 18:39, NASB

> The LORD is my strength and my shield; my heart trusts in Him, and I am helped; therefore my heart exults, and with my song I shall thank Him.
>
> —PSALM 28:7, NASB

> But we have this treasure in earthen vessels, so that the surpassing greatness of the power will be of God and not from ourselves.
>
> —2 CORINTHIANS 4:7, NASB

Do not be afraid. Stand still, and see the salvation of the LORD, which He will accomplish for you today. For the Egyptians whom you see today, you shall see again no more forever. The LORD will fight for you, and you shall hold your peace.

—EXODUS 14:13–14, NKJV

As the mountains surround Jerusalem, so the LORD surrounds his people both now and forevermore.

—PSALM 125:2

I do not fight my enemies in my own strength. My strength comes from the Lord. He is my strength and shield. My heart trusts Him, and He gives me the power to overcome. God trains my hands for war (Ps. 144:1) and He fights for me. Like mountains surrounding a city, God surrounds me with His power and love. I declare victory.

God is my healer and deliverer.

I am the LORD, who heals you.

—EXODUS 15:26

He heals the brokenhearted and binds up their wounds.

—PSALM 147:3

The Spirit of the Sovereign LORD is on me, because the LORD has anointed me to proclaim good news to the poor. He has sent me to bind up the brokenhearted, to proclaim freedom for the captives and release from darkness for the prisoners, to proclaim the year of the LORD's favor and the day of vengeance of our God, to comfort all who mourn, and provide for those who grieve in Zion—to bestow on them a crown of beauty instead of ashes, the oil of joy instead of mourning, and a garment of praise instead of a spirit of despair. They will be called oaks of righteousness, a planting of the LORD for the display of his splendor.

—ISAIAH 61:1–3

By his wounds you have been healed.

—1 PETER 2:24

So if the Son sets you free, you will be free indeed.

—JOHN 8:36

It is for freedom that Christ has set us free.

—GALATIANS 5:1

Whether my wounds are physical or emotional, whether I am sick in body or in soul, God is my healer. I decree that by His wounds I have been healed. God will give me beauty for ashes and heal my heart. I choose to move forward. Neither sickness nor traumatic events will derail my destiny. I will not let a root of bitterness or unforgiveness set in and cause trouble in my life (Heb. 12:15). I refuse to play the victim. I embrace God's healing and deliverance. Whom the Son sets free is free indeed.

God is my provider.

The LORD will guide you always; he will satisfy your needs…and will strengthen your frame. You will be like a well-watered garden, like a spring whose waters never fail.

—ISAIAH 58:11

And my God will meet all your needs according to the riches of his glory in Christ Jesus.

—PHILIPPIANS 4:19

Do not worry about your life, what you will eat or drink; or about your body, what you will wear. Is not life more than food, and the body more than clothes? Look at the birds of the air; they do not sow or reap or store away in barns, and yet your heavenly Father feeds them. Are you not much more valuable than they?

—Matthew 6:25–26

Do not be anxious about anything, but in every situation, by prayer and petition, with thanksgiving, present your requests to God.

—Philippians 4:6

I will not worry about tomorrow, or about what I will eat or wear, because God is my provider. Instead of being anxious, I will present my requests to God. He will supply all my needs.

I know God hears and will answer my prayers.

Ask and it will be given to you; seek and you will find; knock and the door will be opened to you.

—Matthew 7:7

Again, truly I tell you that if two of you on earth agree about anything they ask for, it will be done for them by my Father in heaven.

—Matthew 18:19

This is the confidence we have in approaching God: that if we ask anything according to his will, he hears us. And if we know that he hears us—whatever we ask—we know that we have what we asked of him.

—1 John 5:14–15

I will make my requests known to God because I know He will answer. I know God desires to give good things to me. As I pray in accordance with His will, I know that God hears me and that I have what I ask of Him.

I am anointed, and I have authority over the enemy.

> But you have an anointing from the Holy One, and all of you know the truth.
>
> —1 JOHN 2:20

> I have given you authority to trample on snakes and scorpions and to overcome all the power of the enemy; nothing will harm you.
>
> —LUKE 10:19

I am anointed, and I have been given authority to tread and trample over all that attacks me. I decree that nothing will harm me.

My weapons are powerful.

> The weapons we fight with are not the weapons of the world. On the contrary, they have divine power to demolish strongholds. We demolish arguments and every pretension that sets itself up against the knowledge of God, and we take captive every thought to make it obedient to Christ.
>
> —2 CORINTHIANS 10:4–5

> No weapon formed against you shall prosper.
>
> —ISAIAH 54:17, NKJV

God has provided me with all I need to wage war against the enemy. My weapons have divine power to demolish strongholds. I decree that I will break every barrier and limitation keeping me from becoming the best version of myself. I will accomplish everything God has planned for me. No weapon formed against me shall prosper.

I war with my worship.

> May the praise of God be in their mouths and a double-edged sword in their hands, to inflict vengeance on the nations and punishment on the peoples, to bind their kings with fetters, their nobles with shackles of iron, to carry out the sentence written against them—this is the glory of all his faithful people. Praise the Lord.
>
> —Psalm 149:6–9

> Oh, clap your hands, all you peoples! Shout to God with the voice of triumph!
>
> —Psalm 47:1, nkjv

> When the trumpets sounded, the army shouted, and at the sound of the trumpet, when the men gave a loud shout, the wall collapsed; so everyone charged straight in, and they took the city.
>
> —Joshua 6:20

> I will bless the Lord at all times; His praise shall continually be in my mouth.
>
> —Psalm 34:1, nkjv

My praise and worship is a weapon against the enemy. I will shout in victory, as the Israelites did at Jericho, even before I see the battle won. I will bless the Lord at all times. His praise shall continually be in my mouth. I am a worshipping warrior.

I fast and pray for breakthrough.

> I humbled my soul with fasting, and I prayed with my head bowed on my chest.
>
> —Psalm 35:13, amp

> Is this not the fast that I have chosen: to loose the bonds of wickedness, to undo the heavy burdens, to let the oppressed go free, and that you break every yoke?
>
> —ISAIAH 58:6, NKJV

> However, this kind does not go out except by prayer and fasting.
>
> —MATTHEW 17:21, NKJV

As the psalmist did, I humble my soul with fasting. Through prayer and fasting I will see the bonds of wickedness loosed, heavy burdens undone, and yokes broken. I will receive breakthrough as I deny my flesh through fasting.

I pursue wisdom.

> Whoever walks with the wise becomes wise.
>
> —PROVERBS 13:20

> If any of you lacks wisdom, you should ask God, who gives generously to all without finding fault, and it will be given to you.
>
> —JAMES 1:5

> But the wisdom that comes from heaven is first of all pure; then peace-loving, considerate, submissive, full of mercy and good fruit, impartial and sincere.
>
> —JAMES 3:17

I will seek God's wisdom, and I will speak words of wisdom. I will walk with the wise so I can become wise, and I will ask God for the wisdom that comes from Him, which is pure, peace-loving, and full of good fruit. I will be a wise warrior who responds to my battles as God leads.

I pursue revival.

> Create in me a pure heart, O God, and renew a steadfast spirit within me.
>
> —Psalm 51:10

> Will you not revive us again, that your people may rejoice in you?
>
> —Psalm 85:6

> Repent, then, and turn to God, so that your sins may be wiped out, that times of refreshing may come from the Lord.
>
> —Acts 3:19

I will humbly seek revival, preparing myself through repentance. I ask God to create in me a clean heart and to cause the dry areas in my life to live again (Ezek. 37). I trust God to renew me in Him and refresh my spirit.

I choose victory.

> For the Lord your God is the one who goes with you to fight for you against your enemies to give you victory.
>
> —Deuteronomy 20:4

> But thanks be to God! He gives us the victory through our Lord Jesus Christ.
>
> —1 Corinthians 15:57

> I have told you these things, so that in me you may have peace. In this world you will have trouble. But take heart! I have overcome the world.
>
> —John 16:33

I am a victor, not a victim. I will not live in defeat, because Jesus already won the victory. Whatever fights I face, I will overcome by the power of God.

Notes

INTRODUCTION

1. *Merriam-Webster*, s.v. "ferocious," accessed January 8, 2019, https://www.merriam-webster.com/dictionary/ferocious.

CHAPTER 1—FEROCIOUS FAITH

1. *Merriam-Webster*, s.v. "doubt," accessed January 9, 2018, https://www.merriam-webster.com/dictionary/doubt.

CHAPTER 2—THE GIFT FROM BETRAYAL

1. "Amari Name Meaning," Babynm.com, accessed February 27, 2019, http://www.babynm.com/75680/amari-meaning.php. Amauri's name is from Amari, which in Hebrew means given by God or a miracle from God. We chose to spell it Amauri because my brother Jamar's nickname is Mauri.

CHAPTER 3—PRESS YOUR WAY THROUGH

1. Blue Letter Bible, s.v. "*haptomai*," accessed March 14, 2019, https://www.blueletterbible.org/lang/lexicon/lexicon.cfm?Strongs=G680&t=KJV.

CHAPTER 5—FREE TO BE FEROCIOUS

1. John Eckhardt, *Deliverance and Spiritual Warfare Manual* (Lake Mary, FL: Charisma House, 2014), 8–9.

2. Eckhardt, *Deliverance and Spiritual Warfare Manual*, 9.

3. Eckhardt, *Deliverance and Spiritual Warfare Manual*, 32–33.

4. Blue Letter Bible, s.v. *"ekballō,"* accessed January 15, 2019, https://www.blueletterbible.org/lang/lexicon/lexicon.cfm?Strongs=G1544&t=KJV.

5. *Merriam-Webster,* s.v. "discipline," accessed January 15, 2019, https://www.merriam-webster.com/dictionary/discipline.

6. *Merriam-Webster,* s.v. "dedicated," accessed January 16, 2019, https://www.merriam-webster.com/dictionary/dedicated.

7. *Merriam-Webster,* s.v. "drive," accessed January 16, 2019, https://www.merriam-webster.com/dictionary/drive.

CHAPTER 6—THINK LIKE A WARRIOR

1. Blue Letter Bible, s.v. *"katapausis"* accessed January 16, 2019, https://www.blueletterbible.org/lang/Lexicon/Lexicon.cfm?strongs=G2663&t=KJV.

2. Joyce Meyer, "Living in God's Rest," accessed January 16, 2019, Joyce Meyer Ministries, https://www.joycemeyer.org/everydayanswers/ea-teachings/living-in-gods-rest.

3. *Merriam-Webster,* s.v. "innovation," accessed January 17, 2019, https://www.merriam-webster.com/dictionary/innovation.

4. *Merriam-Webster,* s.v. "innovation."

CHAPTER 7—THE WEAPONS OF A WARRIOR

1. Blue Letter Bible, s.v. *"shabath,"* accessed January 14, 2019, https://www.blueletterbible.org/lang/lexicon/lexicon.cfm?Strongs=H7673&t=KJV.

2. Fox Insider, "'Every Praise': Kidnapper Releases 10-Year-Old Who Won't Stop Singing Gospel Song," FOX News

Network, LLC, April 22, 2014, https://insider.foxnews.com/2014/04/22/%E2%80%98every-praise%E2%80%99-kidnapper-releases-10-year-old-who-won%E2%80%99t-stop-singing-gospel-song.

3. "Ask the Expert: What Makes a Lion Roar?," Cleveland Zoological Society, accessed January 13, 2019, https://www.clevelandzoosociety.org/z/2017/11/30/ask-the-expert-what-makes-a-lion-roar.

CHAPTER 8—THE P PRINCIPLES OF PRAYER

1. *Merriam-Webster*, s.v. "objective," accessed February 28, 2019, https://www.merriam-webster.com/dictionary/objective.

2. *Merriam-Webster*, s.v. "instinct," accessed March 1, 2019, https://www.merriam-webster.com/dictionary/instinct.

3. *Merriam-Webster* (thesaurus), s.v. "forgive," accessed March 1, 2019, https://www.merriam-webster.com/thesaurus/forgive.

CHAPTER 10—FEROCIOUS VICTORY

1. Blue Letter Bible, s.v. "*hypernikaō*," accessed March 1, 2019, https://www.blueletterbible.org/lang/Lexicon/Lexicon.cfm?strongs=G5245&t=KJV.

APPENDIX B—SCRIPTURES AND DECLARATIONS TO AWAKEN THE WARRIOR IN YOU

1. Some of the scriptures and declarations in this appendix were adapted from Michelle McClain-Walters, *Prayers and Declarations for the Woman of God* (Lake Mary, FL: Charisma House, 2018).

My **FREE GIFT** to You:
GET FEROCIOUS!

I'm so happy you read my book. It's so important to stand strong in the face of spiritual attack.

As a thank you, I am offering you a few gifts:

- **E-book:** *Daddy Loves His Girls* **by T. D. Jakes**
- **E-book:** *Help! I'm Raising My Children Alone* **by T. D. Jakes**
- **E-book:** *Ferocious Warrior* **by Cora Jakes-Coleman**

To get these **FREE GIFTS,** please go to:

www.FerociousWarrior.com/gift

Thanks again, and God bless you,

Pastor Cora